TED WILLIAMS:
Seasons of the Kid

TED WILLIAMS:

RICHARD BEN CRAMER
PHOTO EDITING BY MARK RUCKER
PHOTO ESSAYS BY JOHN THORN
INTRODUCTION BY DANIEL OKRENT

PRENTICE
HALL
PRESS

NEW YORK   LONDON   TORONTO   SYDNEY   TOKYO   SINGAPORE

The Seasons of the Kid

Prentice Hall Press
15 Columbus Circle
New York, New York 10023

Library of Congress Cataloging-in-Publication Data

Cramer, Richard Benjamin.
        Ted Williams: the seasons of the kid / text by Richard Benjamin
    Cramer; photo editor, Mark Rucker; introduction, Daniel Okrent;
    photo essay, John Thorn.
              p.   cm.
        ISBN 0-13-515693-9
        1. Williams, Ted, 1918–   . 2. Baseball players—United States—
    Biography. 3. Boston Red Sox (Baseball team)—History.
    I. Rucker, Mark. II. Title.
    GV865.W5C73   1991
    796.357' 092—dc20
    [B]   91-21505

A Baseball Ink Book

Designed by The Knickerbocker Design Group

Manufactured in the United States of America

First Edition

10 9 8 7 6 5 4 3 2 1

PHOTOGRAPHIC PERMISSIONS ON PAGE 256

CONTENTS

ACKNOWLEDGMENTS

First among equals when it comes to expressing our appreciation is Richard Puff of Baseball Ink, who guided this rather elaborate book to completion with production skill, graphic flair, and supreme imperturbability. Alan McKnight and the Knickerbocker Design Group wrapped our efforts in this handsome package.

Paul Aron, our editor at Prentice Hall, conceived this book as a literary portrait rather than just a book for fans; his support and guidance were indispensable throughout its creation. Lucy Salvino, production chief at Prentice Hall, was also invaluable.

Although the providers of photographs are credited at the back of the book, we would like to thank particularly Bill Loughman and Ray Medeiros for generously sharing not only their collections but also their vast knowledge of and affection for Ted Williams. Our gratitude extends also to John Spalding and Ace Marchant for their pictures and helpful recommendations about little-known sources. Steven Gietschier, Director of Historical Records at *The Sporting News*, provided personal assistance and expertise during our visit to the offices of baseball's bible.

Providing speed, savvy, and unfailing good cheer were photo archivists Pat Kelly at the National Baseball Library, Ann K. Sindelar at Western Reserve Historical Society, Frank Kern at San Diego Hall of Champions, and Bill Beeker at Cleveland State University.

On our photo expedition to Ted's home town of San Diego, Phil Lowry, Ellen P. Lowry, and Jay Walker were very helpful. Top quality photographic reproduction was provided by Mike Saporito and Phil Haggerty. In addition, we owe a debt to Andy Strasberg, John Holway, Gertrude Baulis, and Brian Kelleher.

Bill Deane of the National Baseball Library helped us in innumerable ways, from supplying obscure box scores to settling ancient disputes among Williams' several biographers. Larry Ritter, our great friend and colleague, pitched in with his unparalleled, if for him customary, graciousness.

Also deserving of thanks are: Frank Cardillino at Atlantic Typesetting and Terry Cardillino of the Type and Design Center, both of Latham, New York; and Tony Mosca, John Percenti, and Elaine Fiero, for photoduplication services.

Finally, a tip of the cap to the Kid himself, for providing so many thrills and for leading such a fascinating life.

INTRODUCTION

The most famous piece ever written about Ted Williams is certainly John Updike's "Hub Fans Bid Kid Adieu," which originally ran in *The New Yorker*. Updike's chronicle of Williams' last day in uniform, of his home run in his last at bat and his dignified (if diffident) final trip around the bases, has been reprinted often enough to destroy a small forest. It has also stood for three decades as the definitive word on The Kid.

A less well known (but equally compelling) Williams piece was written about the same event, by the journalist Ed Linn for *Sport* magazine. (You can—and should—find it in *The Third Fireside Book of Baseball*, edited by Charles Einstein.) Were it not trite to cite *Rashomon* in such circumstances, I'd cite *Rashomon*. What Updike saw from his seat in the stands was a proud warrior; what Linn saw, in the clubhouse before and after the game, was a bitter, vindictive man beset by unspeakable demons. (These included Williams' least favorite species, sportswriters, as well as a variety of internal gremlins usually categorized only by psychologists.) To fans—Updike, say—Williams was godlike; to those writers like Linn occupationally compelled to follow him, he was something much baser. Read the two pieces in tandem, and you emerge with the conviction that among those things that are truly unknowable, Ted Williams tops the list.

Unless, that is, you turn to Richard Ben Cramer. Cramer is a journalist with a Pulitzer Prize in his satchel, tucked next to ticket stubs from reportorial tours to civil wars in Lebanon, Guatemala, and Afghanistan. I remember meeting him before the third game of the 1986 World Series, when the incubus of doom that accompanies the Red Sox was still hanging out in distant parts of the Back Bay and had not yet occupied the body of Bill Buckner. A shorter version of the text for this book had been published in *Esquire* early that summer; now Cramer was reporting a piece about Peter Ueberroth for the same magazine.

Cramer, whose face can light up like Bill Veeck's scoreboard in the old Comiskey Park, couldn't believe his luck. Like so many other journalists before him, he had figured out a way to set aside (for a time) the weightier work that usually occupied him and turn now toward baseball. Before a World Series game, the mob of press in attendance wanders around the edges of the field during batting practice in little packs, waiting to surround the player or manager who deigns to make himself available for a pregame interview. Not Cramer: standing by the low railing near the visitors' dugout, he simply reveled in his circumstances, grinning with joy and virtually dancing a jig. He reminded me of Walter Huston's old miner in *Treasure of the Sierra Madre*, anticipating the gold in the hills.

Yet Cramer the journalist triumphed over Cramer the fan. His Ueberroth piece, which appeared the following spring, wasn't about the joy and delight of baseball. It was really more of a wrestling match, the supernaturally evasive Ueberroth finally getting pinned by the relentless Cramer. The interview was about drugs and politics and that even more dangerous thing, ambition. Cramer-as-elf had metamorphosed back into Cramer-as-Javert.

I shouldn't have been surprised. A similar thing had happened when Cramer encountered Ted Williams. This is not to say that this wonderful piece of writing is an assault; the reader will surely recognize the writer's regard for his subject (if not—eternally impossible with Williams—the reverse). What Cramer does here is let Ted be himself, let him behave, and thereby nail down the definitive sense of subject that eluded both Updike and Linn. This couldn't have been easy to do. As experienced a profile subject as Williams is, he certainly would know how to erect a protective wall.

But not one so high that it would impede Cramer. With all due respect to both Updike and to Linn, this is the best portrait of baseball's best hitter that anyone has ever written. It merges Updike's awe-struck regard with Linn's piercing iconoclasm, largely by letting some air out of the former and shelving the prejudgement of the latter. And, I should add, by doing one other thing that no else could do: by employing the exceptional skill that belongs to Richard Ben Cramer alone.

This book came into existence because Cramer's original piece, before its adept emendation by the editors of *Esquire*, had never been published anywhere. (*Esquire* should not be blamed; a magazine has to have several rooms in its house, and this one couldn't let Cramer occupy the whole thing.) But we should also bow in the direction of Mark Rucker and John Thorn, respectively responsible for the pictures and their captions and chapter openings.

The debate between the camps of Ruth and Williams over who was baseball's greatest hitter may never be settled (I go with Ted, largely because of the much less hitter-friendly era in which he played). It's almost as unclear who was the better photo subject. Rucker, who is so good at his work that I sometimes feel that he finds pictures that haven't even been taken yet, here surpasses even his excellent work in *The Babe: A Life in Pictures*, his 1988 photodocumentary about Ruth. Ted was never the clown that the Babe was, but he understood the camera just as instinctively. The evidence is here on nearly every page.

John Thorn, whose years of assembling, editing, and publishing baseball books qualify him for national gratitude, provides in the captions a harmonious *basso continuo* for Cramer's melody. All three men (Cramer, Rucker, Thorn) have, I believe, done their best work here. I suppose it's because they're in the same circumstances as those pitchers who had to confront their subject for his two decades in baseball: anything less than your best, and Ted will take you out of the park.

No: even if you have your best, Ted will take you out of the park. Just turn the page and watch it happen.

Daniel Okrent

FOREVER YOUNG

Few men try for the best ever, and Ted Williams is one of those. There's a story about him I think of now. This is not about baseball but fishing. He meant to be the best there, too. One day he says to a Boston writer: "Ain't no one in heaven or earth ever knew more about fishing."

"Sure there is," says the scribe.

"Oh, yeah? Who?"

"Well, God made the fish."

"Yeah, awright," Ted says. "But you had to go pretty far back."

It was in 1939, when achievements with a bat first brought him to the nation's notice, that Ted Williams began work on his defense. He wanted fame, and wanted it with a pure, hot eagerness that would have been embarrassing in a smaller man. But he could not stand celebrity. This is a bitch of a line to draw in America's dust.

In this epic battle, as in the million smaller face-offs that are his history, his instinct called for exertion, for a show of force that would *shut those bastards up*. That was always his method as he fought opposing pitchers and fielders who ganged up on him, eight on one half of the field; as he fought off the few fans who booed him and the thousands who thought he ought to love them, too; as he fought through, alas, three marriages; as he fought to a bloody standoff a Boston press that covered, with comment, his every sneeze and snort. He meant to *dominate*, and to an amazing extent he did. But he came to know, better than most men, the value of his time. So over the years Ted Williams learned to avoid most annoyance. Now in his seventh decade, he has girded his penchants for privacy and ease with a fierce bristle of dos and don'ts that defeat casual intrusion. He is a hard man to meet.

Matinee-idol good looks; a lithe, powerful frame; offhand, unaffected charm; blistering intensity: that was the catalog of the Kid you formed in the first minute you met him. But there was more to the man, far more, and so much of it was visible beneath the thin skin that you were tempted to think you knew him, really knew what made him tick. You didn't.

The big grin, the thundering voice, the hearty thump on the back, the genuine warmth and generous spirit—these are authentic parts of the man inspiring fierce loyalty by those who are permitted to love him. For the rest, not chosen, there is a sign on the fence: KEEP OUT.

This is not to paint him as a hermit or a shrinking flower, Garbo with a baseball bat. No, in his hometown of Islamorada, on the Florida Keys, Ted is not hard to *see*. He's out every day, out early and out loud. You might spot him at a coffee bar where the guides breakfast, quizzing them on their catches and telling them what *he* thinks of fishing here lately, which is, "IT'S HORSESHIT." Or you might notice him in a crowded but quiet tackle shop, poking at a reel that he's seen before, opining that it hasn't been sold because "THE PRICE IS TOO DAMN HIGH," after which Ted advises his friend, the proprietor, across the room: "YOU MIGHT AS WELL QUIT USING THAT HAIR DYE. YOU'RE GOIN' BALD, ANYWAY." He's always first, 8 AM, at the tennis club. He's been up for hours, he's ready. He fidgets, awaiting appearance by some other, any other, man with a racket, whereupon Ted bellows, before the newcomer can say hello: "WELL, YOU WANNA PLAY?" Ted's voice normally emanates with gale force, even at close range. Apologists attribute this to the ear injury that sent him home from Korea. But Ted can speak softly and hear himself fine, if it's only one friend around. The roar with which he bespeaks himself in a public place, or to anyone else, has nothing to do with his hearing. It's *your* hearing he's worried about.

Ted Williams can hush a room just by entering. This he has come to accept as his destiny and his due, just as he came to accept the maddening, if respectful, way that opponents pitched around him (he always seemed to be leading the league in bases on balls), or the way every fan in a ballpark seemed always to watch (and comment upon) T. Williams' every move. It was often said Ted would rather play ball in a lab, where fans couldn't see. But he never blamed fans for watching him. His hate was for those who couldn't or wouldn't *feel* with him, his effort, his exultation, pride, rage, or shame. If they wouldn't share those, then there was his scorn, and he'd make them feel that, by God. These days, there are no crowds, but Ted is watched, and why not? What other match could draw a kibitzer's eye when here's Ted, on the near court, pounding toward the net, slashing the air with his big racket, laughing in triumphant derision as he scores with his killer drop shot, or smacking the ball twenty feet long and roaring, "SYPHILITIC MOTHER OF JESUS!" as he hurls his racket to the clay at his feet.

And who could say Ted does not mean to be seen when he stops in front of the kibitzers, as he and his opponent change sides. "YOU OKAY?" Ted wheezes as he yells at his foe. "HOW D'YA FEEL?... HOW OLD ARE YOU?... JUST WORRIED ABOUT YOUR HEART HA-HA-HAW." Ted turns and winks, mops his face. A kibitzer says mildly: "How are you, Ted?" And Ted drops the towel, swells with Florida air, grins gloriously and booms back:

"WELL, HOW DO I LOOK?...HUH?... *WHAT DO YOU THINK OF TED WILLIAMS NOW?*"

It is another matter, though, to interrupt his tour of life, and force yourself to his attention. This is where the dos and don'ts come in, where matters get tricky. The dos fall mostly to you. They concern your conduct, habits, schedule, attitude, and grooming. It's too long a list to go into here, but suffice it to recall the one thing Ted liked about managing the Washington Senators: "I was in a position where people had to by God *listen*."

The don'ts, on the other hand, pertain to Ted, and they are probably summed up best by Jimmy Albright, the famous fishing guide, Ted's friend since 1947 and Islamorada neighbor: "Ted don't do," Jimmy says, "mucha anything he don't want to."

He does not wait or bend his schedule: "I haven't got my whole career to screw around with you, bush!" He does not screw around with anything for long, unless it's tying flies, or hunting fish, and then he'll spend all day with perfect equanimity. He does not reminisce, except in rare moods of ease. He does not talk about his personal life. "Why the hell should I?"

His standing in the worlds of baseball and fishing would net him an invitation a night, but he does not go to dinners. One reason is he does not wear ties, and probably hasn't suffered one five times in a quarter-century. Neither does he go to parties, where he'd have to stand around with a drink in his hand, "listening to a lot of horseshit." No, he'd rather watch TV.

He does not go to restaurants, and the reasons are several: They make a fuss, and the owner or cook is on his neck like a gnat. Or worse, it's a stream of *sportsfans* (still Ted's worst epithet) with napkins to sign. At restaurants, you wait, wait, *wait*. When Ted wants to eat (about 5 PM), he wants to eat NOW! Restaurants have little chairs and tables, no place for elbows, arms, knees, feet. In Ted's house there is nothing small. Glasses are great double-thick tumblers, forks and knives fill the hand, dishes are continental plates. At restaurants, there's never enough food. Ted eats with a teenager's lust, and if he wants more, he wants MORE! Lastly, restaurants charge a lot and Ted doesn't toss money around. (A few years ago he decided that $2.39 was his top price for a pound of beef. For more than a year, he honed his technique on chuck roast and stew meat. Only an incipient boycott by his friends, frequent dinner guests, finally shook his resolve.)

This last reason is seized upon unkindly by restaurateurs in Islamorada and nearby Keys: "No, he doesn't come in. He's too cheap. He'd go all over town, sonofabitch, and he'd pay by check, hoping they wouldn't cash the check, they'd put it on the wall."

But this is resentment speaking, and it is Ted's lot in life to be misunderstood. Some are put off, for instance, by the unlisted phone, by the steel fence, the burglar alarm and KEEP OUT signs that stud his gates when he swings them shut with the carbon-steel chain and the padlock. But friends think nothing of it. A few have his number, but they don't call, as they know he's got the phone off the hook. No, they'll cruise by; if the gates are unchained, if they see his faded blue truck with the bumper-sign IF GUNS ARE OUTLAWED ONLY OUTLAWS WILL HAVE GUNS, if it's not mealtime and not too late, and there's nothing they know of that's pissing Ted off, well, then... they drive right in.

And this is the way to meet Ted: by introduction of an old friend, like Jimmy Albright. It's Jimmy who knows where to park the car so it won't annoy Ted. It's Jimmy who cautions, as we throw away our cigarettes, that Ted won't allow any smoke in his house. It's Jimmy who starts the ball rolling, calls out "Hiya, Ted!" as the big guy launches himself from his chair and stalks across the living room, muttering in the stentorian growl which passes with him as *sotto voce*: "Now who the hell is THIS?"

He fills the door. "Awright, come on in. WELL, GET THE HELL IN HERE!" He sticks out a hand, but his nose twitches, lip curls at a lingering scent of smoke. Ted's got my hand, now, but he says to Jimmy: "S'that you who stinks, or this other one, too? Jesus! Awright, sit down. Sit over there."

Ted wants to keep this short and sweet. He's in the kitchen, filling tumblers with fresh lemonade. Still, his voice rattles the living room: "D'YOU READ THE BOOK?" He means his memoir, *My Turn at Bat*. "Anything you're gonna ask, I guarantee it's in the goddamn book.... Yeah, awright. I only got one copy myself.

"Where's the BOOK," he yells to Louise Kaufman, his mate. Ted thinks that Lou knows the location of everything he wants. "HEY, SWEETIE, WHERE'S THAT GODDAMN BOOK?"

Lou has raised five sons, so no man, not even Ted, is going to fluster her. She comes downstairs bearing the book, which she hands to Ted, and which he throws to the floor at my feet. He growls: "I want you to read that. Then I'm gonna ask you a *key question*."

I ask: "Tomorrow? Should I call?"

"HELL NO."

Jimmy says he'll arrange a meeting.

Ted says: "HOW'S THAT LEMONADE?"

"Good."

"HUH? IS IT?... WELL, WHAT DO YOU THINK OF ME?"

In the car, minutes later, Jimmy explains that Ted won't talk on the

Ted's boyhood residence at 4121 Utah Street, San Diego, California, as it looks today. The home was exceedingly modest and, with his mother and father gone all day and much of the night, not a place of care and comfort.

phone. "Ted gimme his number twenty-five years ago," Jimmy says. "And I never give it yet to any asshole." We both nod solemnly as this fact settles in, and we muse on the subject of trust. I'm thinking of the fine camaraderie between sportsmen and… wait a minute. Jimmy and Ted have been friends forty years now. Does that make it fifteen years that Ted *didn't* give him the number?

I'm glad it's over. Before anything else, understand that I am glad it's over… I wouldn't go back to being eighteen or nineteen years old knowing what was in store, the sourness and the bitterness, knowing how I thought the weight of the damn world was always on my neck, grinding on me. I wouldn't go back to that for anything. I wouldn't **want** *to go back. I've got problems now. I've always been a problem guy. I'll always have problems…*

—Ted Williams, *My Turn at Bat*

San Diego was a small town, and the Williams house was a small box of wood, one story like the rest on Utah Street. It was a workingman's neighborhood, but at the bottom of the Great Depression, a lot of men weren't working. Ted's father was a photographer with a little shop downtown: passport photos, sailors with their girls; he'd work until nine or ten at night and, still, it wasn't great. Later he got a political job, U.S. marshal, in gratitude for some election favors he'd done for Governor Merriam, and that remained his claim to fame. Ted didn't see much of him. His mother was the strength in the family, a small woman with a will of steel who gave her life to the Salvation Army. She was always out on the streets, in San Diego or south of the border, "The Angel of Tijuana," out fighting the devil drink, selling the *War Cry*, or playing on a cornet, and God-blessing those who vouchsafed a nickel. Sometimes she'd take along her elder boy, and Ted would fidget as hours dragged by. He hated it worse than anything, but he didn't disobey. He was a scrawny kid and shy, and he tried to shrink behind the bass drum so none of his friends would see. There was school, but he wasn't much good there. History was the only part he liked. And then he'd come home, and his mother was out, and sometimes it was ten at night, and Ted and his brother, Danny, were still on the porch on Utah Street, waiting for someone to let them in.

Soon home lost its place at the center of Ted's life. There wasn't much in the little house that could make him feel special. It wasn't the place where he could be the Ted Williams he wanted to be. North Park playground was a block away, and there with one friend, a bat, and a ball, Ted could be the biggest man in the majors. The game he played was called Big League: one kid pitched, the other hit to a backstop screen with a bar across the middle. A ground ball past the pitcher was a single, a liner to the screen below the bar was a double, over the bar was a triple, and a ball that hit the bar and fell before the pitcher caught it—that was a home run. "Okay, here's the great Charlie Gehringer," Ted would announce to himself, as he took his stance. Or

Mrs. May Williams with the ever-present issue of *The War Cry*. She joined the Salvation Army in 1904; it was her mission and vocation until her death in 1961.

sometimes it was Bill Terry, Hack Wilson, or another great man he'd never seen. "Last of the ninth, two men on, two out, here's the pitch... *Gehringer swings!*" Ted swung... *Crack!* Another game-winning shot for the great... *the Great Ted Williams.*

They were just the dreams of a skinny kid, but, oh, he loved to hear about the great men... and not just the athletes, but the great men of history, like the pilot Charles Lindbergh—a hero. Ted saw him once at the stadium. And Ted dreamed of flying. But how could he fly?... He was good at tennis—maybe he'd be *great.* But he broke the gut strings on his racket and a re-string cost thirty-five cents. What good were dreams with a busted racket?... But that bat, the way that ball jumped—that was no dream. He went back to the playground. He went back every day, for years.

The Kid is father to the Man. Here he is at age six, sporting the hated if fashionable Buster Brown coiffure. (The image bears the stamp of photographer Samuel Stewart Williams— Ted's dad.) A decade later he was the star pitcher and slugger of San Diego's Herbert Hoover High School. (*Opposite*) In 1935, as a junior, he batted .586 and the pro scouts took notice. In 1936 he "slumped" to .403.

Lefty O'Doul *(top)* was an inspiration to Ted and something of a role model besides. He, too, started as a pitcher, was pounded hard, and found his calling with the bat. O'Doul had a career batting average of .349 over eleven big-league seasons and, like the Kid, he was a great hitter all the way up to his final at bat: managing Vancouver in the Pacific Coast League in 1956, the 59-year-old Lefty called upon himself to pinch hit. He ripped a triple.

First it was with a friend his own age, then the playground director, Rod Luscomb, a grown man, a 200-pounder who'd made it to the Cal State League. Ted pitched to Luscomb, Luscomb to Ted. At first they'd always tell one another when they were going to throw a curve. But then Ted started calling out: "Don't tell me, just see if I can hit it." *Crack!* Ted could hit it. "Listen, Lusk," Ted used to say, "someday I'm going to build myself a ballpark with cardboard fences. Then, I'm going to knock 'em all down, every darn one, with home runs." But Ted wasn't hitting many homers with his scrawny chest, those skinny arms. Luscomb set him to pushups, twenty, then forty, fifty, then a hundred, then fingertip pushups. Ted did them at home on Utah Street. He picked his high school, Herbert Hoover High, because it was new and he'd have a better chance to make the team. When he made it, he came to school with his glove hung like a badge on his belt. He carried a bat to class. And after his last class (or before), it was back to the playground. Then in darkness, home for dinner, the pushups and the dreams.

There were no major leagues in San Diego. There were hardly any games on the radio; there was no TV. He had no more idea of the life he sought than we have of life on the moon. Maybe less, for we've seen the replays. Ted had to dream it all himself. And how could he measure what he'd give up? He wasn't interested in school, didn't care about cars, or money, or girls. No, if a girl talked to him, he'd run the other way. He felt so awkward, except on the field. There, he'd show what Ted Williams could do. Hoover High went to the state tourney, traveled all the way to Pomona for a doubleheader, and Ted pitched the first game, played outfield in the second, and hit and hit, and Hoover won, and wasn't it great? Ted had shortcake and malted milk, drank eleven bottles of soda. There was an ice cream cart, and Ted ate eighteen Popsicles. His teammates started counting when he got to ten. But Ted didn't mind them making fun. That's how good he felt: him hitting and Hoover winning, and the big crowd. Gee, that's the governor! And Ted found himself in the governor's path, the man who'd tossed his father a job, and he had to say something, and the awkwardness came flooding back, he felt the red in his face. So Ted grabbed tighter on his bat and barked at Merriam: "HIYA GOV!"

At seventeen, as high school closed, he signed with the local team, the Coast League Padres. They offered $150 a month and said they'd pay for the whole month of June, even though this was already June 20. So that was Ted's bonus—twenty days' pay. He didn't care: he was a step closer, and each day was a new wonder.

Ted rode the trains, farther from home than he'd ever been. He stayed in hotels with big mirrors, and he would stand at a mirror with a bat, or a rolled-up paper, anything—just to see his swing, how he looked. He got balls from the club, so many that his manager, Frank Shellenback, thought Ted must be selling them. No, Ted took them to his playground, got Lusk and maybe a kid to shag flies, and hit the covers off those balls. And he ate on meal money, anything he wanted, until the owner, Bill Lane, called him: "Kid, you're heading the list." And Ted knew he was only hitting .271, so he said, "What list?" Lane growled: "The overeaters list. It's supposed to be $2.50 a day." But Ted was six-three now, and lucky if he weighed 150. He *had* to be stronger. He growled back: "Take it outa my pay."

Best of all, there were major leaguers, real ones, to see. They were old by the time they came to the Coast League, but Ted watched them, ate them with his eyes, measured himself against their size. Lefty O'Doul was managing the San Francisco Seals, and he was one of the greats: he had hit .398 and 32 homers for the Phils in 1929. Ted stopped Lefty on the field one day. He had to know: "Mr. O'Doul, please... what should I do to be a good hitter?" And Lefty said: "Kid, the best advice I can give you is don't let anybody change

When he reported to the Padres in 1936, Ted had reached his full height of 6'3", but he weighed only 148 pounds. Where *did* the power come from? Not from the physique, although that would become impressive, but from technique: God-given talent harnessed with hard, hard work.

① WAITING FOR BALL, WILLIAMS STANDS MOTIONLESS
② AS BALL NEARS PLATE, HE GETS READY FOR SWING
③ JUDGING PATH OF THE BALL, WILLIAMS CONNECTS
④ WILLIAMS KEEPS EYES FOCUSED ON THE HIT BALL
⑤ HIS POWER RELEASED, WILLIAMS FOLLOWS THROUGH
⑥ HE CLOSES EYES ONLY AFTER FINISHING THE SWING

CONTINUED ON NEXT PAGE 43

you." Ted walked around on air. After that, in bad times, he'd hear O'Doul's voice telling him he'd be okay. The bad times were slumps. If Ted couldn't hit, the world went gray. In his second year with San Diego, Ted hit a stretch of 0-for-18. He hung around the hotel in San Francisco, moping. He didn't know what to do with himself. He got a paper and turned to the sports. There was an interview that day, with O'Doul. The headline said: "WILLIAMS GREATEST HITTER SINCE WANER." And Ted thought: I wonder who this Williams is?

It was a newspaper that told him, too, about Boston buying his contract. The Red Sox! Ted's heart sank. It was a fifth-place club, and as far away as any team could be: cold, northerly, foreign. Still, it was big league, wasn't it?

He had to borrow $200 for the trip east; there were floods that spring, 1938. He got to Sarasota about a week late. And when he walked into the clubhouse, all the players were on the field.

"Well, so you're the kid."

It was Johnny Orlando, clubhouse boy. The way Johnny told it, he'd been waiting for this Williams. "Then, one morning, this Li'l Abner walks into the clubhouse. He's got a red sweater on, his shirt open at the neck, a raggedy duffel bag. His hair's on end like he's attached to an electric switch. If anybody ever wanted a picture of a raw rookie, this was the time to take the shot.

"'Where you been, Kid?' I asked him. 'Don't you know we been working out almost a whole week? Who you supposed to be, Ronald Coleman or some-body, you can't get here in time?'..." Johnny gave Ted a uniform, the biggest he had in stock. But as Ted grabbed for a couple of bats, his arms and legs stuck out, the shirttail wouldn't stay in the pants.

"Well, come on, Kid," Johnny said, and he led the beanpole out to the field. From the first base stands, a voice yelled: "Hey, busher, tuck your shirt in! You're in the big leagues now."

Ted wheeled around, face red. "Who's that wise guy up in the stands?" Johnny told him: "That's Joe Cronin, Kid, your manager." Ted put his head down and made for the outfield. It wasn't the reception he'd expected, but at least he had his nickname. Everyone heard Johnny show him around: "Look here, Kid. Go over there, Kid. Hey, we'll need a uniform long enough for the Kid." It stuck right away; it was a role he knew. And soon, Joe Cronin would fill the spot Rod Luscomb had held in Ted's life. Cronin was only thirty-one, but that was old enough. He was a hitter and a teacher, manager, counselor, and Ted was ever the Kid.

Cronin had come from Washington, one of the Red Sox' imported stars. The owner, Tom Yawkey, was buying a contender. Along with Cronin, the Hall of Fame shortstop, Yawkey had raided Washington for Ben Chapman, a speedy right fielder and a .300 hitter. From the Browns, Yawkey got Joe Vosmik, a left fielder who would hit .324. From the A's, Yawkey bought two old greats, Lefty Grove and Jimmie Foxx, along with Doc Cramer, another .300 hitter for center field.

These were the finest hitters Ted had seen. He couldn't take his eyes off

the batter's box. But the presence of all those hitters in camp meant one thing of terrible import to Ted: no nineteen-year-old outfielder was going to break in, not that year, and the veterans let Ted know it. Vosmik, Chapman, and Cramer, rough old boys, all of them, made sure he had his share of insults, called him busher, laughed in his face. Ted lasted about a week, until the club broke camp for the first game in Tampa. Ted said to Cronin: "Am I on the list, Joe?" Cronin said: "Why don't you look at the damn board like everybody else and *see* if you're on the list."

Ted wasn't on the list. He was headed to Daytona Beach, where the Minneapolis farm team trained. He was boiling. And the shame welled up in his craw, turned to rage. He yelled to the veteran outfielders: *"I'll be back. And I'll make more money in this fucking game than all three of you combined."*

When he walked to the bus stop with Johnny Orlando, he asked: "How much you think those guys make?" And Johnny said: "I don't know, twelve-five, maybe fifteen thousand apiece." Ted nodded, his mouth set in a grim line. He had his salary goal now. Then he borrowed $2.50 from Johnny for the bus trip to the minors.

Joe Cronin was Ted's teammate, manager, general manager, and enduring friend. Not riding him too hard or reining in his rookie excesses—though in later years Ted wished he had done more to protect him from the press—Cronin gave the Kid a chance to grow up.

In 1938, his one year with the Minneapolis Millers, Ted tore up the American Association, winning the Triple Crown with a batting average of .366, 43 home runs, and 142 RBIs. But his play in the outfield and on the basepaths drove manager Donie Bush (*inset*, shown in 1922 when he managed the Washington Senators) to distraction, drink, and despair. Maybe the Kid was going to be the game's next great star, but the comparisons offered by newsmen around the Triple-A circuit were not to Babe Ruth but to Babe Herman—or to Ring Lardner's "Elmer the Great." It is hard to fathom today, but as he rose to the majors Ted was universally regarded as a screwball.

He was back the next spring, this time with batting records and tall tales preceding him. In Minneapolis, he'd led the league in everything: average, home runs, runs batted in, runs scored, screwball stunts, and ink consumed. There were tales of his conduct in the outfield, where he'd sit down between batters, or stand with an imaginary bat in his hand, taking his stance, watching his leg stride, watching his wrists break, watching everything except balls hit to his field. If he did notice a fly ball, he'd gallop after it, slapping his ass and yelling, "HI-HO SILVER!" He was nineteen, and fans loved him. But if there was one boo, the Kid would hear it, and he'd try to shut that sonofabitch up for good. Once, when a heckler got on him, Ted fired a ball into the stands—and hit the wrong guy. That was more than the manager,

poor old Donie Bush, could stand. He went to the owner, Mike Kelley, and announced: "That's it. One of us goes. It's him or me." Kelley replied, quick and firm: "Well, then, Donie, it'll have to be you."

By the time Ted came back to Sarasota, the Red Sox were banking on him, too. They traded Ben Chapman, the right fielder who'd hit .340 the year before. Ted told himself: "I guess that shows what they think of ME." It was like he had to convince himself he was really big league now. Even after a good day, three-for-four, he'd sit alone in the hotel with the canker of one failure eating at him. If he screwed up, or looked bad, the awkwardness turned to shame, the shame to rage. As the team headed north, barnstorming, Ted was hitting a ton, but it wasn't enough. At the first stop, Atlanta, Johnny Orlando pointed out the strange right field wall—three parallel fences, one behind the other. Johnny said: "I saw Babe Ruth hit one out over that last fence…" Ted vowed right there he'd do it, too. But next day, he couldn't clear even one fence. Worse still, he made an error. In the seventh, he put the Sox up with a three-run triple, but that wasn't enough. He had to show what Ted

Ted poses in Sarasota with two fortuitously nick-named Red Sox hopefuls of 1938, Red Nonnenkamp *(left)* and Red Daughters. Nonnenkamp was the one who made the club. Next spring the Kid went to camp assured of a job.

Williams could do! When he struck out in the ninth, he went to right field seething. Then a little popup twisted toward his foul line. Ted ran and ran, got to the ball, dropped it, then booted it trying to pick it up. Rage was pounding in him. He grabbed the ball and fired it over those right field walls. By the time the ball hit on Ponce de León Avenue and bounced up against a Sears store, Cronin had yanked Ted out of the game.

Even Ted couldn't understand what that rage was to him, why he fed it, wouldn't let it go. He only knew that the next day in Atlanta, he smashed a ball over those three walls and trotted to the bench with a hard stare that asked Johnny Orlando, and anyone else who cared to look: Well, what do you think of the Kid now?

He had a great first year in the bigs. On his first Sunday at Fenway Park, he was 4-for-5 with his first home run, a shot to the bleachers in right-center, where only five balls had landed the whole year before. There were nine Boston dailies that vied in hyperbole on the new hero. TED WILLIAMS REVIVES FEATS OF BABE RUTH, cried a headline after Ted's fourth game.

1939, Opening Day lineup for Bosox: Doc Cramer, center field; Joe Vosmik, left field; Ted Williams, right field (yes, he played right the whole year); Jimmie Foxx, first base; Joe Cronin, shortstop; Jim Tabor, third base; Bobby Doerr, second base; Gene Desautels, catcher; Jack Wilson, pitcher. Fast company, but the Kid was a match for it.

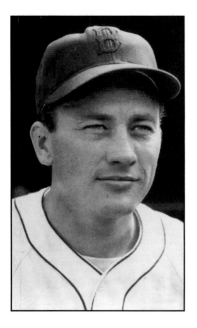

From every town, he wrote a letter to Rod Luscomb with a layout of the ballpark and a proud X where his homer had hit. He was always first to the stadium and last to leave after a game. He took his bats to the post office to make sure they were the proper weight. He quizzed the veterans mercilessly about the pitchers coming up. "What does Newsom throw in a jam? How about Ruffing's curve?" It was as if he meant to ingest the game. He only thought baseball. On trains, he'd never join the older guys at poker games or drinking bouts. At hotels, it was always room service, and Ted in his shorts, with a bat, at a mirror. His roomie was Broadway Charlie Wagner, a pitcher with a taste for fancy suits and an occasional night on the town. One night, at 4 AM, Wagner was sleeping the sleep of the just when, *wham, CRASH*, he's on the floor, with the bed around his ears, and he figures it's the end. He opens his eyes to see the beanpole legs, then the shorts, and then the bat. Ted's been practicing, and he hit the bedpost. Does he say he's sorry? No, doesn't say a damn thing to Wagner. He's got a little dream-child smile on his face and he murmurs to himself: "Boy, what power!"

He ended up hitting .327 and led the league in runs batted in, the first time a rookie ever won that crown. He finished with 31 home runs, at least one in each American League park. There was no Rookie of the year award, but Babe Ruth himself put the title on Ted, and that seemed good enough. His teammates were always pounding his back; the writers heaped on praise. And whenever fans cheered, Ted waved his cap like a cavalryman on a charge.

And after the season, he didn't go home. San Diego had lost its hold. His

parents were getting a divorce, and that was pain he didn't want to face. He didn't want to see his troubled brother. He didn't want to see the crummy little house with the stained carpet and the chair with the hole where the mice ate through. He had a car now, a green Buick worth a thousand bucks. He went to Minnesota. There was a girl there he might want to see. Her dad was a hunting guide and he could talk to her. And there were ducks to hunt, as many as he wanted. He could go where he wanted. And do what he wanted. He was twenty-one. And Big League.

Everybody knew 1940 would be a great year. Ted knew he'd be better: now he'd seen the pitchers, he knew he could do it. Tom Yawkey sent him a contract for $10,000, double his rookie pay. "I guess that shows what they think of ME," Ted told himself, and vowed he'd be worth every dollar. He was already worth more. In his first year, attendance rose ten percent. Now, the Red Sox moved the right field fence twenty feet closer to

"Boy, what power!" That's the line that sent Broadway Charlie Wagner (*top left*) crashing to the floor at 4 AM. "Boy, what style!" That's what the rookie imagines the photogs are thinking as he poses artistically. And despite Ted's modest sentiments quoted below by Boston *Post* cartoonist Bob Coyne, a Back Bay writer said of the rookie, "If his noodle swells another inch, he won't be able to get his hat on without a shoe horn."

home plate. It was still no cheap shot at 380, but if Ted had poled fourteen out of Fenway as a rookie, just *think* what he'd do with the new fence! And fans were thinking: The Sox had come in second to the Yanks two years in a row. For the first time in two decades, since the Babe went to New York, there was pennant fever in Boston.

No one thought about this, but pitchers had seen Ted, too. And this time around, no one was going to try to blow a fastball by him, or throw him anything fat. Cronin was having an off-year and "Double X" Foxx was getting old and would never again be the batting champ. So the pressure fell to Ted. If they pitched around him and he got a walk, that wasn't enough—the Sox needed hits. If he got a hit, it should have been a homer. A gaggle of bleacherites started riding Ted. And why not? They could always get a rise. Sometimes he'd yell back. Or he'd tell the writers: "I'm gonna take raw hamburger out to feed those wolves." The papers rode the story hard: O Unhappy Star! Then he told the writers: "Aw, Boston's a shitty town. Fans are lousy." Now the papers added commentary, pious truths about the Boston fans as the source of Ted's fine income. So Ted let them have it again: "My salary is peanuts. I'd rather be traded to New York." That did it. Now it wasn't just a left field crowd riding Ted. It was civic sport: *He doesn't like Boston, huh? Sure, the Kid can hit. But who does he think he is?*

And Ted rode himself harder. If he hit a crummy two-hopper to the right side, no one at Fenway could be more disgusted than Ted. More than once, he pulled up cursing, halfway to first, didn't run it out. And then, once again, Cronin yanked him from the game and, once again, the papers went to town on Ted. Writers would work the clubhouse, trying to *explain* the Kid. Big Jimmie Foxx, a hero to Ted, said: "Aw, he's just bein' a spoiled boy." The great Lefty Grove said if Williams didn't hustle, he'd punch him in the nose. Of course, all that made the papers. Now when the writers came back to his locker, Ted didn't wait for questions. "HEY, WHAT STINKS?" He'd yell in their faces. "HEY! SOMETHING STINK IN HERE? OH, IT'S YOU. WELL, NO WONDER WITH THAT SHIT YOU WROTE." So they made new nicknames for him: Terrible Ted, Teddy Tantrum, the Screwball, the Problem Child. Fans picked it up and gave him hell. It didn't seem to matter what he *did* anymore. Ted read the stories in his hotel room, and he *knew* he was alone. Sure, he read the papers, though he always said he didn't. He read the stories twenty times; he'd recite them word for word. He'd pace the room and seethe, want to shut them up, want to hit them back. He didn't know how.

And Ted would sit alone in the locker room, boning his bats, not just the handle, like other guys did, but the whole bat, grinding down on the wood, compressing the fiber tighter to make it tougher, harder, tighter, tighter. He would sting the ball, he'd show them. He'd shut them up. Jesus, he was trying. And he was hitting. Wasn't his average up? Sure, only seven homers at home, but he couldn't win a pennant alone. Wasn't he leading the league in runs? He was doing it, like he'd taught himself, like he'd dreamed. Wasn't that enough? What the hell did they want? What did they want him to be?

What else could he be? Some players tried to help, to ease him up a bit. Once, Ted gave Doc Cramer a ride, and they were talking hitting, as Ted always did. It was at Kenmore Square that Cramer said: "You know who's the best, don't you? You know who's the best in the league? You are." And Ted never forgot those words. But neither could he forget what was written, just as he couldn't forget one boo, just as he'd never forget the curve that struck him out a year before. Why didn't they understand? He could never forget.

And one day, he made an error, and then struck out, and it sounded like all of Fenway was booing, and he ran to the bench with his head down, the red rising in his face, the shame in his belly, and the rage. Ted thought: *These are the fans I tipped my cap to?* He vowed to himself: *Never again.* And he could not forget that either.

Lou is in a Miami hospital for heart tests. Ted says I can drive up with him. He figures we'll talk, and he'll have me out of his hair. We start from his house and I wait for him on the porch, where a weary woman irons. The woman is filling in for Lou and she's been ironing for hours. Ted may wear a T-shirt until it's half holes and no color at all, but he wants it just so. The woman casts a look of despair at the pile, and announces: "She irons his *underpants*."

Ted blows through the back door and makes for the car, Lou's Ford,

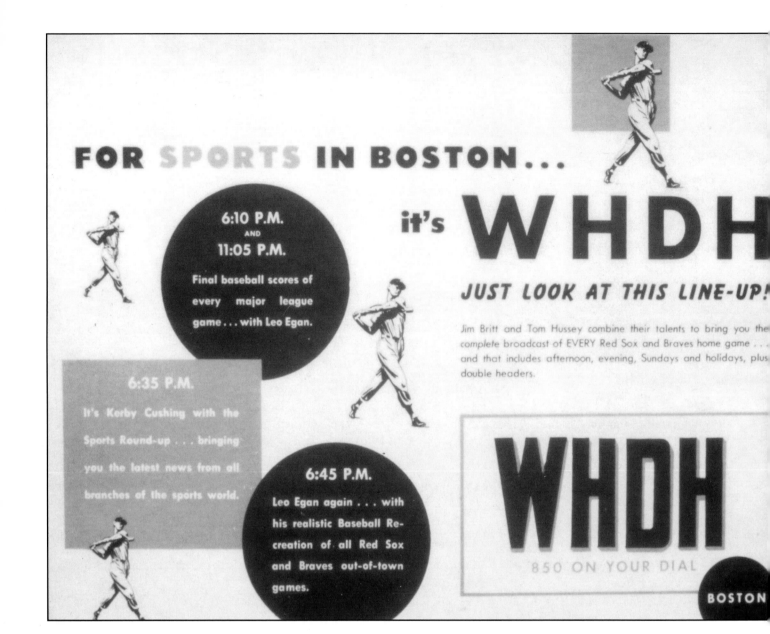

which he proclaims "a honey of a little car, boys!" When Ted puts his seal of
judgment on a thing or person, by habit he alerts the whole dugout. We are
out of Islamorada on the crowded highway, U.S. 1, the only road that perse-
veres to these islets off the corner of the country, when Ted springs his key
question. "You read the book? Awright. Now we're going to see how smart
YOU are. What would YOU do to start, I mean, the first goddamn thing now,
the first thing you see when you're sitting in the seats and the lights go off,
how would YOU start the movie?"

Ted is considering a film deal for *My Turn at Bat*. He is working the
topic of moviedom, as he does anything he wants to know. Now as he pilots
the Ford through Key Largo, he listens with a grave frown to some possible
first scenes. "Awright. Now I'll tell you how it's supposed to start, I mean how
the guy's doing it said…. It's in a fighter plane, see, flying, from the pilot's eye,
over KOREA, maybe Seoul. And it's flying, slow and sunshine and then *bang*
WHAM BOOOOMMM the biggest goddamn explosion ever on the screen, I

mean BOOOOOMMM. And the screen goes dark. DARK. For maybe ten seconds there's *NOTHING.* And then when it comes back there's the ballpark and the crowd ROARING... and that's the beginning."

"Sounds great, Ted."

"Does it? LOOKIT THIS ASSHOLE NOW. I wonder where he's goin'. Well, okay, he's gonna do *that.* Well, okay—I'm passing too. Fuck it." Ted is pushing traffic hard to be at the hospital by two, when Lou's doctors have promised results from the heart tests. He is trying to be helpful, but he's edgy.

"How long have you and Lou been together?"

"Oh, I've known Lou for thirty-five years. You shouldn't put any of that shit in there. Just say I have a very wonderful friend, that's all. I wouldn't put anything in about her. Shit."

"Yeah, but it makes a difference in how a man lives, Ted, whether he's got a woman or not..."

"Boy, that Sylvester Stallone, he's really made something out of that Rocky, hasn't he?..."

"So Ted, let me ask you what..."

"LOOK, I don't wanta go through my personal life with YOU, for

Ted's struggle with the press obscured the larger war, the one between the intensely private man and the relentlessly public hero. He hated the media version of Ted Williams because, artificial though it was, he couldn't simply ignore it: he had either to reject it or to live up to it. What other people thought of him—even the faceless crowd—*mattered.*

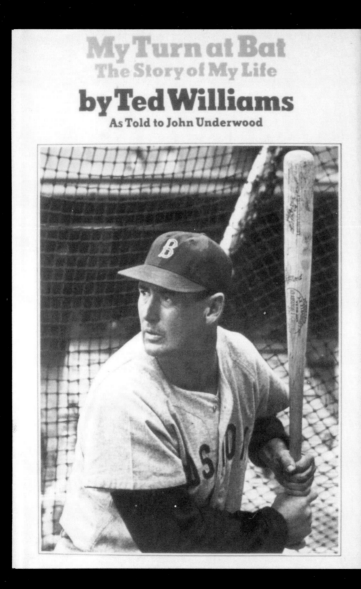

My Turn at Bat
The Story of My Life
by Ted Williams
As Told to John Underwood

christsake. I won't talk to you about Lou, I won't talk to you about any of it. You came down here and you're talkin' about me, as I'm supposed to be different and all this and that…"

"Do you think you're different?"

"NO, not a damn bit. I'm in a little bit different POSITION than people. I mean, I've had things happen to me that have, uh, made it possible for me to be different. DAMN DIFFERENT in some ways.

"Everybody's not a big league ballplayer, everybody doesn't have, uh, coupla hitches in the service, everybody hasn't had uh, as much notoriety about 'em as I had ALL MY LIFE, so…"

"So…"

"I wanna go NORTH. I'm gonna go up here and go further down. I made a mistake there, GODDAMMIT, HOW THE HELL DO I GET ON THE FUCKIN' THING? I'll make a U turn and go down…"

"Ted, I think you were more serious about living life on your own terms than… "

"Well, I wanted to be alone at times. It was the hustle and the bustle of the crowd for nine months a year. So certainly, I wanted a little more privacy and a little more quiet, a little more tranquility around me. This is the fucking left we wanted."

"Yeah, but it's not just privacy, Ted. I'm not trying to make it seem unnatural. But what you toss off as a little more privacy led you *off* the continent, so far off in a corner that…"

"Well, lemme tell you about Koufax. He got through playin' baseball, he went to a fuckin' little shitty remote town in Maine, and that's where he was for five years. Everybody thought he was a recluse, he wasn't very popular just 'cause he wanted to be alone and he finally moved out. Lemme tell you about Sterling Hayward, Hayden. HELL of an actor. And still he wanted to be ALONE, he wanted to TRAVEL, he wanted to be on his BOAT GOIN' TO THE SOUTH SEAS. Christ, uh, look at Hemingway, he went to Key West fifty, sixty years ago. So, see, that's not way outa line!… I guess I'll take a right, that oughta do it. 874, do you see 874 anyplace? Go down here till I get to Gilliam Road, or some goddamn thing… Fuck, 874's where I wanted to go, but looked like it was puttin' me back on the fuckin' turnpike, shit… So, you know, seeking privacy and, uh, seeking that kind of thing… what road is this?"

"We're on Killian… So privacy, you don't think that's what?"

"*Unusual* for Christsake. Shit."

"I don't think it's unusual either."

"WELL, YOU'RE MAKIN' A PROJECT OUT OF IT!"

"No, I don't think it's unusual… You don't think you're exceptionally combative?"

"Nahh, me? Not a bit. Hell, no. THAT SAY KENDALL? Does it? Well, I made a hell of a move here. HELL of a move! See, 874 comes right off there, hospital's down here…"

"You're a half hour early, too."

"I felt a lot of people didn't like me," Williams wrote in his autobiography, *My Turn at Bat*. He wasn't going to let *them* do that to *him*. Anticipating rejection, he would make himself so disagreeable as to ensure it, and so deny its hurt. In this fine book, written with John Underwood, Ted at last allowed the outsiders in.

After a sophomore season in which he failed to meet his own lofty goals, especially in home runs, the Kid began his glory year of 1941 by fracturing his ankle in spring training. This may have been a lucky break, since for the first two weeks of the regular season it limited him to pinch hitting duty, thus reducing his plate appearances in the cold weather which he despised. By mid-June he was hitting .436. Then came the All Star Game and the two-out, ninth-inning, three-run homer which he has always described as "the biggest thrill I ever got in baseball."

"Here it is, right here, too. Best hospital in Miami. Expensive sonofabitch, boy. Christ. Boy, I'm all for Medicare. And I've always thought that, ALWAYS thought that. Shit. WELL, WHERE ARE YOU GOING? Where ARE you going, lady? CUNT!" Ted takes the parking space vacated by the lady and tells me he'll be back in an hour.

When he comes back, he has good news about Lou: all tests are negative, her heart is fine. "Gee, I met the big cardiovascular man, he came in and I met him." Ted sounds twenty years younger.

He's walking to the car when a nurse passes. "GEE, WASN'T IT A SHAME," Ted suddenly booms, "THAT ALLIGATOR BIT THAT LITTLE GIRL'S LEG OFF?" He casts a sly sideward glance at the nurse to see if she's fallen for his favorite joke.

"Honey of a little shittin' car!" he sings out as we hit the road. Now there is no fretting with traffic. Ted makes all the turns. Along the way, he sings forth a monologue about cars, this car, this road, this town of Homestead, that house, his house, the new house he's planning in central Florida, up on a hill, second highest point in the whole goddamn state, what a deal he's getting there, Citrus Hills, HELL of a deal; about his hopes for his kids, his daughter, Claudia, only fourteen, who lives in Vermont with her mother, Ted's third wife, who was too much of a pain in the ass to live with, but gee, she's done a hell of a job with those kids, HELL of a job; the little girl is an actress, she had the lead in the Christmas play and she was so good, the papers up there all said "She Bears Watching," SHE BEARS WATCHING, and her brother, Ted's boy, John Henry, he's picking colleges now, he's a good boy and Ted's critical, but he can't see too much wrong with that boy, and even the big daughter, Bobby Jo, she's straightening out pretty good now, she's thirty-nine already and still can bust Ted's chops pretty good, boys, but she's straightening out; and these little islands, there's bonefish here, and it used to be wonderful, years ago when there was NOTHING, NOTHING, except a few of the best fishermen God ever made, and a narrow road, bay and sea, just a little shittin' road, and some women who weren't half bad on the water or off it either, and the world here was empty and the water was clear and you could have a few pops of rum, maybe get a little horny, go see friends, that's all there was here, a few friends, thirty, thirty-five years ago, when this place was young, when he first fished with Jimmy and he met Lou…

"Gee, I'm so fuckin' happy about Louise," Ted says. "Goddamn, she's a great person. Have more fun with her than… Goddamn."

They booed in Boston? Well, not in Detroit, the 1941 All Star Game, with all the nation listening in. Ted doubled in a run in the fourth, but the National League still led 5–3, going into the ninth. Then an infield hit, a single, a walk, a botched double play, and here it was: two out, two on, bottom of the ninth. *Here's the great Ted Williams.* Claude Passeau, the Cubbie on the mound, sends a mean fastball in on his fists. *Williams swings!* When the ball made the seats, Ted started jumping on the basepath.

Joe DiMaggio met him at home plate, Bob Feller ran out in street clothes, Cronin jumped the box seat rail, the dugout emptied. The manager, Detroit's Del Baker, kissed him on the forehead. They carried the Kid off the field.

He was showing them all now: after the All Star break, Ted was still hitting more than .400. Sure, guys hit like that for a month, but then tailed off. No one had hit like that for a year, not since the twenties, and each day the whole country watched. Every paper ran the box score: *Will'ms, LF, 1-for-3, 2-for-4...* Writers from New York joined the Sox. *Life Magazine* brought its new stop-action camera to photograph Ted in his shorts, swinging like he did in front of the mirror. Ted was on national radio: "Can you keep it up, Kid?" He always replied that there was no such thing as a .400 hitter anymore, but then, back in his room, he'd add: *No such hitter... except me.* But it was murderous pressure. By the end of August, he was slipping, almost a point a day. Then he'd gather strength: *Will'ms, LF, 2-for-4...* On the last day, the Sox would have two games in Philadelphia. Ted had slipped to .39955. The way they round off averages, that's still .400. Cronin came to Ted on the eve of the twin bill and offered: "You could sit it out, Kid, have it made." But Ted said he'd play.

That night, he and Johnny Orlando walked Philadelphia. Ted stopped for milkshakes, Johnny for whiskey. Ten thousand people came to Shibe Park, though the games meant nothing. Connie Mack, the dour and penurious owner of the A's, threatened his players with fines if they eased up on Williams. But Ted didn't need any help. First game, he got a single, then a home run, then two more singles. Second game, two more hits: one a screaming double that hit Mr. Mack's right field loudspeaker so hard that the old man had to buy a new horn. In all, Ted went 6-for-8, and .406 for his third season. That night, he went out for chocolate ice cream.

Who could tell what he'd do the next year: maybe .450, the best *ever*, or break the Babe's record of sixty homers. He got a contract for $30,000, and he meant to fix up his mother's house in San Diego. He'd have more money than he'd ever expected in his life. He was the toast of the nation. But then the nation went to war.

Ted wanted to play. He'd read where some admiral said we'd kick the Japs back to Tokyo in six months. What was that compared to hitting? A lawyer in Minnesota drew up a plea for deferment, and Ted okayed the request: he was entitled, as his mother's support. When the local board refused deferment, the lawyer sent it up for review by the presidential board. That's when the papers got it. In headlines the size of howitzer shells, they said Ted didn't want to fight for his country. Teddy Ballgame just wanted to play.

Tom Yawkey called to tell him he could be making the mistake of his life. The president of the American League told Ted to go ahead and play. Papers ran Man on the Street polls. In Boston, Ted was bigger news than war in the Pacific. When he went to spring training, Joe Cronin said he'd be on his own with fans. "To hell with them," Ted spat. "I've heard plenty of boos." Still, he

After his .406 season prompted a contract offer of $30,000, Ted figured he easily would be able to provide for his mom. As her sole support, he was entitled to a III-A deferment, and on appeal he won it. But he was booed unmercifully throughout April of 1942 (unlike Joe DiMaggio, Stan Musial, and the many others who played ball that year). In May he signed up for Naval Aviation training, to begin at the baseball season's end.

Ted Williams knew he was born to hit a baseball, but he never dreamed he would enjoy piloting an airplane as much as he did. He enjoyed it so much, in fact, that in 1943-45 he had hardly any appetite for baseball. In the photo below, the "B" on his cap is not for Boston but for the Bronson Field team of the aviation training center at Pensacola, Florida, 1944.

read every letter. He remembered the venomous ones that said he was an ingrate or a traitor. The one that hurt most said nothing at all: it was just a blank sheet of paper—*yellow* paper.

Opening Day in Boston, reporters sat in the left field stands, out there with soldiers and sailors, to record their reaction to Ted. The Kid treated the day as a personal challenge. His first time up, two on, two strikes, he got a waist-high fastball and drilled it into the bleachers. All the fans rose to cheer, servicemen among them. The Kid was back, and Fenway was with him. "Yeah, ninety-eight percent were for me," Ted said, later, as he scraped his bat. A writer said: "You mean a hundred percent. I didn't hear a boo." Ted said: "Yeah… except a couple of kids in the left field stand, and a guy out in right. I could hear them."

In May, he enlisted for Navy wings and that shut up most of the hecklers. Still, he was always in a stew of contempt for some joker who said something unfair. It seemed Ted courted the rage now, used it to bone his own fiber. Now there was no awkwardness, no blushing before he blew. It was automatic, a switch in his gut that snapped on and then, watch out for the Kid. One day in July, a fan in left was riding Ted pretty hard. Ted came to bat in the fifth: he took a strange stance and swung late, hit a line drive, but well foul into the left field seats. Next pitch, again he swung late, hit another liner, but this stayed fair—and Ted didn't run, barely made it to second. Cronin yanked him out of the game and fined him $250 for loafing. But Ted wasn't loafing, he was just caught by surprise. He'd been trying to kill the heckler with a line drive foul.

Ted loved the service, its certainty and ease. He never had a problem with authority. It was drawing his own lines that gave him fits. He had his fears about the mathematics, navigation problems, and instrument work. But at Amherst College, where the Navy started training, he found his mind was able, and he was pleased. He loved the way the college felt, the old walls and classroom smell. He had, for the first time, a whiff of another life.

And he loved the feel of an airplane. At Pensacola, in the Florida wilds, the others in his flight group would follow the prescribed training routes. But if Ted saw a river below, he'd drop in a screaming dive to treetops, and follow every wiggle of the water in his plane. He got his wings near the top of his class and signed on as an instructor to stay at Pensacola. He was happy and good at his job. Strangely, in uniform, he was freer than before.

On the day he was commissioned (second lieutenant, U.S. Marines) he married that daughter of the hunting guide, Doris Soule, from Minnesota. Now, for the first time, he'd have a house, a place on the coast near the base. And now, on the off-days, he'd scrape up some gas stamps, grab his flyrod, find a lonesome canal, and lose himself in a hunt for snook. Back at the base, Ted would grab a new cadet and put him in the back seat of his SNJ, and the new guy of course was goggle-eyed, flying with *Ted Williams*, and Ted would make his plane dance over the coast; then he'd dive and point, and yell to the cadet: *"That's where the Kid fished yesterday."*

Orders came through slowly. What base commander would give him up as ornament and outfielder? At last he got combat training at Jacksonville (where he broke test records), and packed up for the Pacific. But Ted was just getting to Hawaii when Japan folded. So he packed up again for Boston, and now he felt he was going to war.

He came back like he owned the game. Opening Day, 1946, in Washington, after a three-year layoff: *crack*, a 400-foot home run. And then another and another, all around the league. By the All Star break in '46, after half a year, he was hitting .365, with 27 home runs. In the All Star Game, Ted alone ruined the National League: four straight hits, five runs batted in, two homers, the second against Rip Sewell, whose famous "eephus" (a lob with an arc twenty feet high) had never been hit out of any park.

And the Red Sox were burying the American League. Tom Yawkey's millions were paying off. The team as a whole hit .300, and Ted was hammering the right field walls. In the first game of two in Cleveland, he hit three home runs, one a grand slam when the Sox were behind 5–0, the second with two on to tie the game, the third in the bottom of the ninth, to win, 11–10. As Ted came up in the second game, Cleveland's manager, Lou Boudreau, started moving men: the right fielder backed toward the corner; the center fielder

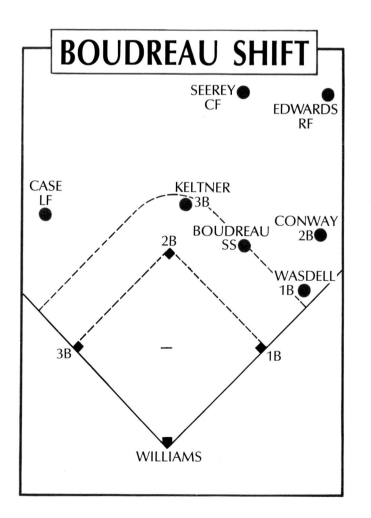

BOUDREAU SHIFT

The Boudreau Shift in its original, radical form, as devised in 1946. The third baseman did not play behind second base but instead played a normal second sacker's position. The Shift could not be employed when a runner was on second base, and it was imprudent even in a nonstealing situation such as bases loaded. All the same, it was stacked against Williams often enough over the rest of his career, and certainly cost him points off his batting average.

played the wall in right-center; the third baseman moved behind second; and
Boudreau, the shortstop, played a deep second base; the second baseman
stood in short right field, and the first baseman played behind his bag. There
were eight men on one half of the field (the left fielder was alone on the other),
and Ted stood at home plate and laughed out loud.

There had never been anything like it. He had bent the nature of the
game. But he would not bend his own, and slap the ball for singles to left. He
hit into the teeth of the Shift, and when he slumped, and the Red Sox with
him, the papers started hammering Ted again, his pride, his "attitude." At
last, against the Shift in Cleveland again, Ted sliced a drive to the wall in left-
center, and slid across the plate with an inside-the-park home run, the first
and last of his career. And that won the Sox their first pennant since 1918. But
the headlines didn't say, "Ted Homers," or even "Sox Clinch." Instead, eight-
column banners revealed that Ted stayed away from the champagne party.

"Ted Williams," Dave Egan wrote in the *Record*, "is not a team man." And when St. Louis pulled the Shift in the Series and held Ted to singles, 5-for-25, the new banner read: WILLIAMS BUNTS. And the Red Sox lost the Series, the first and last of his career, and after the seventh game in St. Louis, Ted went to the train, closed his compartment, put his head down, and cried. When he looked up, he saw the crowd on the platform watching him through the window. The papers wrote: "Ted Williams cannot win the big ones." Fans voted him number two in a poll for Flop of the Year.

I t seemed like Ted couldn't laugh anymore, not in a ballpark. He said he was going to Florida to fish. He didn't want to see a bat for months. Soon that was a pattern: one year, before spring training, he tucked in a week on the Everglades. Next year, it was a month. Year after that, longer. In early 1948, the papers discovered that Doris was in a Boston hospital to deliver Ted's first child. But where was the big guy? In Florida? FISHING? The mothers of Boston pelted the press with angry letters. "To hell with them," Ted said. He didn't come north for two days. And two days after he did come, he was back fishing. In two years, he'd moved Doris and his daughter, Barbara Joyce, to a house in Miami, the first he'd ever owned. But

In the 1946 World Series against the Red Sox, the St. Louis Cardinals employed a variant of the Boudreau Shift named for their manager, Eddie Dyer. In Game 3 Williams, who had pulled into the teeth of the Shift in the American League all year, crossed up everyone by bunting.

Ted always loved to fish and as he moved around the country he went after the strongest, gamest fish the locale had to offer. He tried his hand at yellowtail and barracuda in the Pacific; muskie in the midwest (as in the photo below, taken on a fishing tour in Hayward, Wisconsin); snook in the Everglades of Florida; bonefish in the Keys; tarpon in the Gulf; and Atlantic salmon on the Miramichi River in New Brunswick, Canada.

he never stayed home there either. He was after fish. He heard about some men in the Keys catching bonefish with light fly tackle. When Ted went to try this new sport, he found a love that would last longer than any marriage.

The Keys were deserted—their railroad was wrecked by a hurricane in 1935. There were only a few thousand souls on one road that ran for a hundred miles; the rest was just mangrove and mosquitoes, crushed coral islands and shining water. In Islamorada—a town of one store, a bar, a restaurant, one gas pump—a few fishing guides, led by Jimmy Albright, were poling their skiffs over shallows that only they knew, hunting bonefish and inventing an art as they went along. These were Ted's kind of men, who'd sneer or scream at a chairman of the stock exchange if he made a lousy cast. Islamorada was a strange meritocracy: if you could not handle a rod, play a fish, tie a fly, or cast a line eighty feet through the wind, you were no one in this town.

Ted could do it all, brilliantly. The guides didn't make much fuss about his fame, but they loved his fishing. His meticulousness and fussy detail work, always an oddity at Fenway Park, was respected here as the mark of a fine angler. Ted had the best tackle, best reels, best rods, the perfect line; his lures were impeccable. He'd work for hours at a bench in his house, implanting balsa plugs with lead, so they'd sail off a spinning rod just so, then settle in

the water slowly like a fly. He could stand on the bow of a skiff all day, watching the water for signs of fish, and soon he was seeing them before the guides. His casts were quick and long; his power was immense. And he played his fish with relentless pressure. He never seemed to snap a line, never tangled up; his knots were sure, his knowledge grew, and he always wanted to know *more*. He'd question Jimmy relentlessly and argue every point. But if you showed him something once, he never needed showing again. He fished with Jimmy week after week, and one afternoon, as he stood on the bow, he asked without turning his head: "Who's the best you ever fished?" Jimmy said a name, Al Mathers. Ted nodded, "Uh-huh," and asked another question, but he vowed to himself: "He don't know it yet, but the best angler he's had is me."

Every winter, he'd fish the flats, then head north to make his appearance at the Boston Sportsmen's Show. He'd spend a few days doing flycasting stunts and then take a couple of hours, at most, to tell Tom Yawkey what he ought to be paid, and pose for pictures as he signed his new contract. His salary was enormous. He was the first to break Babe Ruth's $80,000 record. Ted didn't care for the money as much as the record. It was history now that was the burr on his back. The joy was gone but not the dream.

Every day, every season, he was still first to the ballpark, where he'd strip to his shorts and bone his bats; still first out to the cage, where he'd bark his imaginary play-by-play: "Awright, Detroit, top of the ninth… Trout on the

Whatever Ted does seems to draw a crowd: talk, hit, fish, tie a fly—all are done with that characteristic, magnetic intensity. Fly-tying has always been a way for him to relax, but Ted even relaxes intensely.

Ted signs a contract for 1947 with Red Sox general manager Eddie Collins, who in 1936 had extracted a promise from San Diego owner Bill Lane to sell the skinny seventeen-year-old outfielder to the Red Sox. Collins' sharp eye and baseball knowledge brought him a Hall of Fame career as a second baseman, and he obviously had a nose for talent.

mound... Here's the pitch!" Then back to his locker for a clean shirt and up at a trot to the dugout, to clap a fierce eye on the pitcher warming up, to pick apart his delivery, looking for any weakness. Johnny Pesky hit ahead of Ted in the lineup. When Pesky was due to lead off, he'd sprint in from shortstop to grab his bat. Otherwise, left fielder Williams would beat him into the dugout, and out to home plate, where he'd yell: "COME ON, YOU LITTLE SHIT! GET OUT HERE AND BAT!"

No, Ted would not give up on one game, a time at bat, a single pitch. No one since Ruth had hit so many home runs per time at bat. No one in the league hit like Ted, year after year: .342, .343, .369, .343... It seemed he never broke a bat at the plate, but he broke a hundred in the clubhouse runway. If he failed at the plate he'd scream at himself, "YOU GODDAMN FOOL..." and bash his bat on the runway cement, while the Red Sox in the dugout stared ahead with mute smiles. Once after a third strike he smashed the one-inch water pipe to the cooler with his bare fists. No one could believe it until the flood began. And on each Opening Day, Ted would listen to the

national anthem and he'd feel hair rise on the back of his neck and his hands would clench like they did on the bat, and he'd vow to himself: "This year, the best EVER."

In the 1950 All Star Game, he crashed against the outfield wall to catch a drive by Ralph Kiner. His elbow swelled while he played eight innings (and got a single to put his team ahead). The elbow was shattered, with thirteen chips off the radius. Surgeons thought he was through, but Ted returned in two months. His first game back, once again: *crack!* A home run, and 4-for-4. But Ted could tell as weeks went by that the elbow was not the same. The ball didn't jump off his bat anymore. So all next winter, Ted stayed in the Keys, where he poled a skiff, hunting bonefish and rebuilding his arm. He was pushing thirty-four now; if he could keep his strength, use his time…

But then, after the '51 season, he was called back to the Marines, drafted for a two-year hitch in Korea. It seemed his time was up.

In the first inning of the 1950 All Star Game in Chicago's Comiskey Park, Ted crashed against the left field wall while hauling in a long drive off the bat of Ralph Kiner. He fractured his elbow and missed most of the rest of the season. He had come into the midsummer classic with 25 homers and 83 RBIs. "I was never the same hitter again," Ted said. He never threw as well again, either.

Everything stopped when the Kid was at the bat. That perfect swing was irresistible to players and fans alike. And, although Ted was slow to comprehend it, so was he. On April 30, 1952, the Fenway faithful gave Ted a day to mark his final game before his callup by the Marines. Ted was presented with a Cadillac. He presented the fans with a tip of the cap—his only such gesture between 1940 and his retirement twenty years later—and a characteristic home run in his final at bat to win the game.

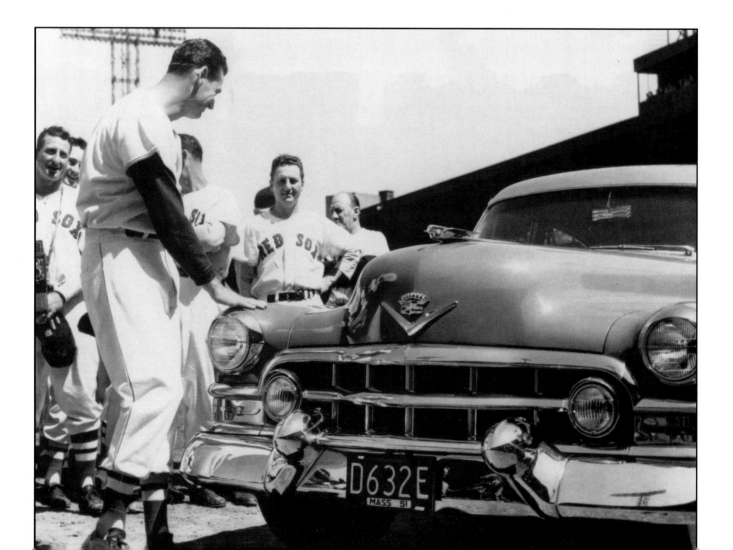

The smile belies the anger, the bitterness over being recalled at the age of thirty-four. All the same, he was an active Marine again, he was going to do his job, and he wasn't going to bitch about it.

Ted's living room has a wide white armchair, into and out of which he heaves himself twenty times a day; the chair has a wide white ottoman onto which he'll flop, as whim dictates, one or both of his big legs. It is from this chair that he roars commands and inquiries, administering the house and grounds. Across the room, a big TV shows his "National Geographic Specials." At his side, a table holds his reading and correspondence. At the moment, these piles are topped by *Yeager: An Autobiography*, and teachers' reports on his son, John Henry, from a prep school in Vermont. To Ted's right, ten feet away, there's a doorway to the kitchen, through which Lou can supply him and let him know who that was on the phone. To his left and behind, a grand picture window affords a view of a patio, his dock, some mangroves, and weather on the Florida Bay. (Ted was always interested in weather, not only for fishing, wherein it is crucial, but for baseball, where wind could defeat him. Each morning, he'd call Fenway from his hotel bed to ask Cronin: "Where's the wind blowing, Joe?" At last, Cronin tired of this and told him: "Up the street, you sonofabitch. Why don't you go out and see?") Finally, ahead and to the right, in a distant semicircle, there are chairs and a couch for visitors.

"NOW WE'RE GONNA SEE HOW MUCH YOU KNOW, SONOFABITCH,"

Ted is shouting at Jack Brothers. Jimmy Albright is there, too, and since both are guides and talking fishing with Ted, everyone is shouting.

"Rumer. R-U-M-E-R!" Brothers contends he is spelling the name of the first spinning reel. But Ted has hurled himself up to fetch a fishing encyclopedia, and now he's back in the chair, digging through the book to the section on spinning. Just so things don't get boring, he says, "Where'd you get that HAIRCUT? D'you have to PAY FOR IT?"

Ted and Jimmy began this colloquy during the Truman administration. Jack helped heat it up when he drifted down from Brooklyn, a few years after the war, before Islamorada got its second restaurant or first motel, not to mention the other ten motels, the condos, gift shops, Burger King, or the billboard that proclaims: SPORTFISHING CAPITAL OF THE WORLD.

"Here. HERE! 'Mr. Brown began importing SPINNERS, starting with the LUXAR...' THE LUXAR. HERE! WANNA SEE? GO AHEAD, SONOFABITCH!"

"Yeah, but that don't say the first spinning reel *manufactured*." Brothers grins in triumph. "You and your damn books! Sonofabitch."

Ted explodes. "This is the goddamn HISTORY, Brothers.... NOT A FUCKING THING ABOUT RUMORS, RHEUMERS, RHOOOMANS... I GUESS YOU DIDN'T KNOW MUCH ABOUT SPINNING REELS, DID YOU?"

Ted is always the one with the books. He wants *answers*, not bullshit. Ted

That pedagogical streak on display again: Ted gives a few aeronautical pointers to Marine reservists at Cherry Point, North Carolina, September 1952.

is always reading history, biography, fact of all kinds. He doesn't like much made of this, as he's tender on the subject of his education. Once in a camp in Africa, while he and his coauthor, John Underwood, gazed at the night sky, Ted turned from the stars and sighed: "Jeez, I wish I was smart like you."

Now he reports to his friends on his college tours with his son, John Henry: "So we get to Babson and I like it. Babson's a pretty good school, boys. HELL of a school, but, uh, they got dorms, boys and girls all in one dorm, see, and I look on the walls and they're written all over, 'Fuck This' and 'Fuck That.' I'm thinking, gee, right out there on the walls, it just seemed, you know…"

"Liberal?" Jimmy suggests.

"Well, I like to see a place with a little more standards than *that*. So we get to Bates. Beautiful. We got this German girl to show us around, see? And she was a smart little shit, two languages, and she's telling us what she's studying, a smart little shit! She give us the tour, see, and John Henry loved Bates, LOVED it. We get back to the office and she goes out. I don't know, she musta told someone, some of her friends, who she just showed around, see? Then somebody *told* her. She didn't know, see…

"Well, a minute later, she's back with some kid and he says, 'OH, Mr. Williams!' and 'OH' this and 'OH' that. And *then* we start talking. And how about *this*, how about *that*, and how would John Henry like to come for a *weekend*, get the feel of the place, you know, and how about THAT, and would we like to see THIS, and I guess…"

Ted stops for a moment and thinks to himself. He doesn't really have to finish the thought for his friends, who can see him beaming in his big chair. So he just trails off, almost to himself:

"… Boy mighta thought the old man wasn't gonna… you know, around a college… . Well!"

The mayor and the Red Sox held a day for Ted when he left for flight school. Three weeks into the '52 season, at Fenway, they gave him a Cadillac, and made a donation to the Jimmy Fund, a charity for sick children which Ted supported. They gave him a Ted Williams Memory Book, with signatures of four hundred thousand fans. For his last at bat, bottom of the seventh, he gave them a two-run homer to win the game, 5–3. He threw a party that night, at his Boston hotel. The crowd was mostly cooks and firemen, bellhops, cabbies, ice cream men. Ted never liked a smart crowd. Smart people too often asked: "Oh, was your father a ballplayer?" "Oh, what did your mother do?" Ted didn't like to talk about that.

He was just Captain Williams, U.S. Marines, at his flight base at Pohang, Korea. He had a shed for a home and a cot with inner-tube strips for springs. The base was a sea of mud, the air was misty and cold, and he was always sick. He was flying close air support, low strafing and bombing runs over enemy lines. His plane was a jet now, an F-9 Panther, but he just couldn't get much joy from flying. He was in and out of sick bay. Doctors called it a virus, then pneumonia, but his squadron was short of pilots, so he always flew.

On one bombing run, north of the thirty-eighth parallel, Ted lost sight of the plane ahead. He swung out to find him and dropped through clouds. When he came out, he was much too low. The North Koreans sent up a hail of bullets. Ted's plane was hit and set afire. The stick stiffened and shook in his hand; his hydraulics were gone. Every warning light was red. The radio sputtered and quit. A marine in a nearby plane was signaling frantically at the back of Ted's plane. He was trying to signal: "Fire! Bail out!" But Ted's biggest fear was ejecting; at six-three, wedged in as he was, he was sure he'd leave his kneecaps under his gauges. So they climbed and the other pilot led him to a base. Ted hauled his plane into a tight turn, and he felt the shudder of an explosion. One of his wheel doors had blown out. Now he was burning below, too. He made for a runway with fire streaming thirty feet behind. Koreans in a village near the base saw his plane and ran for their lives. He tried to blow his wheels down; only one came out. He had no dive breaks, air flaps, nothing to slow the plane. He hit the concrete runway at 225 miles an hour and slid for almost a mile, while he mashed the useless brakes so hard he almost pushed them through the floor, as he screamed *"STOP YOU DIRTY SONOFABITCH STOP STOP STOP."* When the F-9 stopped skidding, he somersaulted out the hatch and slammed his helmet to the ground. Two Marines grabbed him on the tarmac and walked him away as the plane burned to char.

He was flying the next day, and the day after. There weren't enough pilots to rest a man. Ted was getting sicker, weak and gaunt, bags under his eyes, and soon his ears were so bad he couldn't hear the radio. He had flown thirty-nine missions and won three air medals when they sent him to a hospital ship off the coast. Doctors sent him on to Hawaii, and then to Bethesda, Maryland, where at last they gave him a discharge. His thirty-fifth birthday was coming up, he was tired and ill. He said he didn't want to do anything,

much less suit up to play. But Ford Frick, the commissioner, invited him to the
'53 All Star Game, just to throw out the first ball.

So Ted went to Cincinnati, sat in a sport coat in the dugout. Players
greeted him like a lost brother; even Ted couldn't hear a boo in the stands.
Tom Yawkey was there and Joe Cronin, and they worked on the Kid. The
league president asked him to come back; the National League president, too.
Branch Rickey sat him down for a talk; Casey Stengel put in a plea. Ted went
to Bethesda to ask the doctors, and then he told the waiting press to send a
message to the fans at Fenway: "Warm up your lungs." He took ten days of
batting practice and returned with the Red Sox to Boston. First game, Fenway, bottom of the seventh: pinch-hit home run.

Ted Williams became the greatest old hitter. In two months,
upon his return from Korea, he batted .407 and hit 13 home runs, one
in every seven at bats. For the next two years, he led the league in average
(.345 and .356), but injuries and walks robbed him of the titles: he didn't get
the minimum four hundred at bats. In 1956, he lost the title in the season's
last week to twenty-four-year-old Mickey Mantle (who finished with .353 to
Ted's .345). The next year, Mantle had an even better season, but Ted, at age
thirty-nine, pulled away and won, at .388, more than twenty points ahead of
Mantle, more than sixty points ahead of anyone else. With five more hits (say,
the leg hits that a younger man would likely get), it would have been a .400
season. As it was, it stood as the highest average since his own .406, sixteen
years before. In 1958, Ted battled for the crown again, this time with a team-

In 1953 Ted returned to
active duty in the baseball
wars and hit home runs at a
phenomenal clip. Hopes
were high for a banner
season in 1954, but ten
minutes after stepping on the
field for his first day of
spring training, he dove for a
liner, tumbled, and
fractured his shoulder. By
mid-decade he would have
to contend for the American
League spotlight with the
equally fragile Mickey
Mantle. (*Overleaf*)

mate ten years his junior, Pete Runnels. They were neck and neck in September, but then, once again, Ted pulled away to win at .328. For the final fifty-five games of the season (including one on his fortieth birthday), he batted .403.

He accomplished these prodigies despite troubles that would have made most men quit. In 1954, he made spring training for the first time in three years, but he wasn't on the field a minute before he fell, lunging for a line drive, and broke his collarbone. He was out six weeks and had a steel bar wired into his clavicle. (First day back, twin bill in Detroit: two home runs, a double, five singles, seven RBIs, 8-for-9.) In 1955, he was out of baseball as the season began, while Doris alleged in divorce court that he'd treated her with "extreme cruelty" and constant profane abuse. When Ted finally got a settlement, Boston papers ran the story under two-inch headlines: TED GETS DIVORCE, complete with a "box score" on the money, the house, the car, and "Mrs. Ted's" custody of Bobby Jo. (First day back, Fenway Park: home run.) In 1956, Ted came forth with his "Great Expectorations." In a scoreless game with the Yankees, in front of Fenway's largest crowd since World War II, he was booed for making an error, and he let fans know what he thought of their affections: he spat toward the right field stands and spat toward the left, and when the fans rained more boos on his head, he leapt out of the dugout again and sprayed all around. "Oh, no, this is a bad scene," Curt Gowdy, the Sox broadcaster, mourned to his microphone. Tom Yawkey heard the game on radio, and Ted got a $5,000 fine (tying another Babe Ruth record). Boston writers said Ted ought to quit "for the good of the Sox and the Game." But Ted was in the next lineup, for Fenway's first Family Night, and at his appearance, fans gave him a five-minute ovation. (He then hit a home run in the bottom of the eighth and clapped his hand over his mouth as he crossed home plate with the winning run.) In 1957, flu knocked him flat and stuck him in his hotel for seventeen days in September. He came back to hit four consecutive home runs. In 1958, ptomaine from bad oysters wrecked Opening Day; then he injured an ankle, pulled a muscle in his side, and hurt his wrist twice. In September, after a called third strike, Ted threw his bat and watched in horror as it sailed into the stands and clonked a gray-haired lady on the head. (The lady turned out to be Gladys Heffernan, Cronin's housekeeper, who only wanted to know, as they carried her out: "Why are they booing Ted?") Ted sat in tears in the dugout and had to be ordered to his place in left field. Again, the writers demanded his scalp. ("He has betrayed all those who defended him," Jimmy Cannon wrote on a national wire.) And over the next twenty at bats, Ted hit .500.

In fact, he did quit at least once a year, and writers "washed him up" a dozen times. Each time they did he'd come back harder, "just for the pleasure," as he told one writer, "of ramming it down your throat." That was about the nicest thing he'd say. In these greatest years, the switch in his gut was always on. The spitting, the "gestures," bats flung—that was the least of it. The Red Sox gave him a single room, and barred the press from the clubhouse for two hours before each game. But it wasn't outside annoyance that

Doris Soule Williams leaves the Dade County Courthouse on May 9, 1955, after obtaining her decree of divorce.

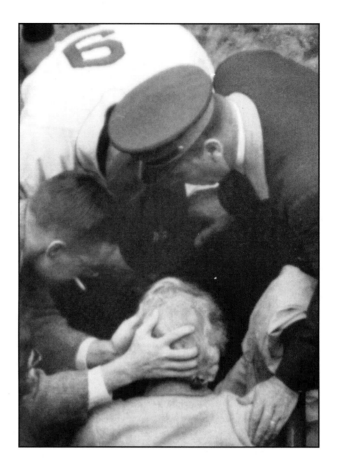

was fueling Ted's rage. He'd wake up in the middle of the night, screaming obscenities in the dark. He kept himself alone and pushed away affection. There were plenty of women, Lou Kaufman foremost, who would have loved to help. But Ted would say: "WOMEN?" and then he'd grab his crotch, "ALL THEY WANT IS WHAT I GOT RIGHT HERE." Now the press didn't cover just explosions on the field. The *American* wrote him up for shredding a telephone book all over the floor when a hotel maid failed to clean his room. "Now tell me some more," wrote Austen Lake, "about Ted's big, charitable, long suffering spirit." Roger Kahn, in the *New York Times*, reported a typical locker scene when Ted was asked about Billy Klaus, the shortstop, who was hitting so well now, after a bad year. "'You're asking *ME* about a BAD YEAR?' The strong voice rose to a shout. 'Mister, I can see you don't know very much about baseball, if you're asking me about a bad year. OLD T.S.W., HE DON'T HAVE BAD YEARS... .'"

But old Ted had a terrible year in 1959. A pain in his neck turned to stiffness, and he was in traction for three weeks. When he came out, he could barely turn his head to look at the pitcher. His average languished below .300 for the first time in his career. For the first time, he was benched for not hitting. ("Rested," the manager, Billy Jurges, insisted.) The sight of The Kid at the plate was pathetic; even the papers softened. They started summing up his career, treating him like an old building menaced by the wrecking ball. He finished at .254 and went to see Tom Yawkey. "What do you think you should do?" Yawkey said, and that burned Ted up. He might have retired if Yawkey had offered a contract. But no one was going to make him retire. No, Ted said he meant to play, and Yawkey, who loved the Kid, offered to renew his contract: $125,000, the highest ever. No, Ted said, he'd had a lousy year, and he wanted a cut. So Ted signed a contract for $90,000, and came back one more time.

Opening Day, Washington: a five-hundred-foot home run. The next day, another, then another. He slammed his five-hundredth in Cleveland, and passed Lou Gehrig and Mel Ott. Only Jimmie Foxx and Babe Ruth would stand ahead of him on the all-time list. At age forty-two, Ted finished his year with 29 homers and an average of .316. Talk revived that Ted might be back. But this was really quits. On his last day at Fenway, a headline cried: WHAT

Ted always said it: There's nothing like a game of pepper to fine-tune that hand-eye coordination. Why don't today's players do it?

WILL WE DO WITHOUT TED? And though the day was dreary and the season a loss, ten thousand came to cheer and hear him say good-bye. There was another check for the Jimmy Fund and, this time, a silver bowl. And Ted made a speech that said, despite all, he felt he was lucky to play for these fans. And when he came up in the eighth and they stood to cheer, he showed them what Ted Williams could do. He hit a Jack Fisher fastball into the bullpen in right field, over the fence that the Sox had moved for him twenty years before. And he thought about tipping his cap as he rounded first, but he couldn't—even then, he couldn't forget—so he ran it straight into the dugout and wouldn't come out for a bow.

Now it was no hobby: Ted fished harder and fished more than any man around. After his divorce from Doris, he'd made his home in Islamorada, bought a little place on the ocean side, with no phone and just room for one large man and his gear. He'd wake before dawn and spend the day in his boat on the flats, and then come in, maybe cook a steak, maybe drive off to a Cuban or Italian joint where they served big portions and left him alone. Then, back home, he'd tie a few flies, oil his reels, and be in bed by ten. He kept it very spare. He didn't even have a TV. That's how he met Louise. He wanted to see a Joe Louis fight, so Jimmy took him over to Lou's big house. Her husband, Bob, was a businessman from Ohio, and they had a TV, they had everything. Lou had her five kids, the best home, the best furniture, the best car, and the best guides. Though she wasn't a woman of leisure, she was a pretty good angler, too. She could talk fishing with Ted. Yes,

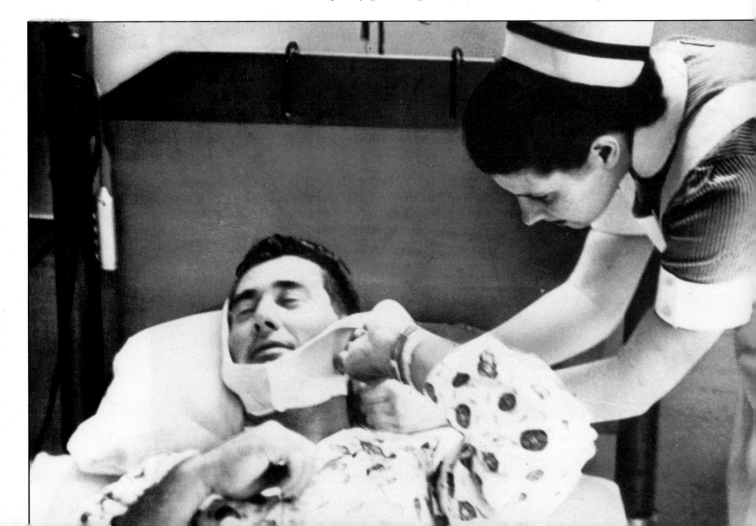

they could talk. And soon, Lou would have a little money of her own, an inheritance that she'd use to buy a divorce and a life of her own. She wanted to do for herself, she said. And there was something else: "I met Ted Williams," Louise said. "And that was the most wonderful thing I ever saw in my life."

Now Ted's life was his to make, too. He signed a six-figure deal with Sears, to lend his name to their line of tackle, hunting gear, and sporting goods. Now, when Hurricane Donna wrecked his little house on the ocean, he bought his three-bedroom place on the bay, near Louise's house. Now he bought a salmon pool on the Miramachi, in New Brunswick, Canada, and he fished the summer season there. In Islamorada, he was one of the few with his own skiff for the flats. He was out every day, fall, winter, and spring, and he treated it like hitting: he wanted the most and the biggest—bonefish, tarpon, salmon; he called them the Big Three. He wanted a thousand of each and kept books on his progress. He thought fishing and talked fishing and taught fishing at shows for Sears. He felt the joy of the sport, still. But now there was something else: the tightness, the need, the switch that clicked when he'd get a hot fish that ran with his lure and broke it off: Ted would slam his rod to the deck, or break it in half on the boat. "HERE, YOU LOUSY SONOFABITCH…" He'd hurl the rod into the bay. "TAKE THAT, TOO."

He married again in 1961, a tall blonde model from Chicago, Lee Howard. They'd both been divorced, and they thought they'd make a go. Ted brought her down to the Keys. But he still wasn't staying home: he'd be out at dawn without a word on where he was going or what he had planned, and then he'd come home, sometimes still without words. Or sometimes, there was only rage and Lee found she was no match. After two years, she couldn't take it. Her divorce petition called it "constant obscene criticism." She added: "I couldn't do anything right. If we went fishing, he would scream at me, call me a —— and kick the tackle box."

So Ted found another woman, one to meet him, fire for fire. Her name

No, he would not go out with a whimper, but with a bang. The Kid came back to hit .316 in 1960, capping his final season with a heroic home run. Forty-two years of age might be near the end of baseball's truncated timeline, but there was a lot more life to be lived. There was romance (a marriage in 1961 to model Lee Howard); there was fishing (especially salmon); there was business (the Ted Williams line of sporting goods for Sears); and there was even to be a return to baseball, as manager of the Washington Senators.

was Dolores Wettach, a tall, large-eyed former Miss Vermont. He spotted her across the aisle on a long plane flight. He was coming back from fishing in New Zealand. Dolores had been in Australia, on a modeling assignment for *Vogue*. He wrote a note: "Who are you?" He wadded it up, tossed it at her. She looked him over, tossed one back: "Who are *you*?" He tossed: "Mr. Williams, a fisherman," and later told her his first name was Sam. It wasn't until their third date she found out he'd done anything but fish. When he found out she was a farm girl who loved the outdoors as much as he, he figured he'd met his match. In a way, he had. She learned to fish, she could hunt, could drink, could curse like a guide. And when they fought, it was toe to toe, and Ted who slammed out of the house. They had a son, John Henry, and a daughter, Claudia. But that didn't stop the fights, just as it never did with Bobby Jo, the first daughter he'd had with Doris. Ted used to tell his friends he wasn't cut out for family life. He was sick at heart when Bobby Jo left school and didn't go to college. He would seethe when any woman let him know that there must be more. What the hell did they want? When Dolores became his third divorce, Ted was through with marriage.

The second marriage didn't work out. The third time—to Dolores Wettach—was not the charm, either, but the union did produce a daughter, Claudia, and a son, John Henry. Here, mother and six-month-old son in March 1969; opposite, father and son a year later, when Ted was in his second campaign as manager of the Senators.

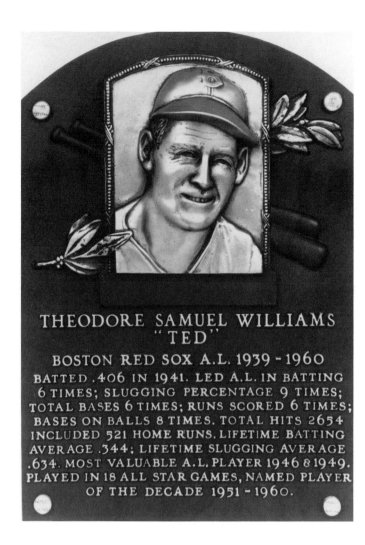

THEODORE SAMUEL WILLIAMS
"TED"
BOSTON RED SOX A.L. 1939-1960
BATTED .406 IN 1941. LED A.L. IN BATTING
6 TIMES; SLUGGING PERCENTAGE 9 TIMES;
TOTAL BASES 6 TIMES; RUNS SCORED 6 TIMES;
BASES ON BALLS 8 TIMES. TOTAL HITS 2654
INCLUDED 521 HOME RUNS. LIFETIME BATTING
AVERAGE .344; LIFETIME SLUGGING AVERAGE
.634. MOST VALUABLE A.L. PLAYER 1946 & 1949.
PLAYED IN 18 ALL STAR GAMES, NAMED PLAYER
OF THE DECADE 1951-1960.

Ted made the Hall of Fame in 1966. His old enemies, the writers, gave him the largest vote ever. So Ted went north to Cooperstown, and made a short speech outside the Hall. Then he went back to Florida. He never went inside. They gave him a copy of his plaque. It listed his .406 year, his batting titles, slugging titles, total bases, walks, home runs. It didn't say anything about the wars, the dream, the rage, the cost. But how much can a plaque say?

There are no statistics on fans, how they felt, what they took from the game. How many of their days did Ted turn around? How many days did he turn to occasions? And not just with hits: There was a special sound from a crowd when Ted got his pitch, turned on the ball, whipped his bat in that perfect arc—and missed. It was a murmurous rustle, as thousands at once let breath escape, gathered themselves, and leaned forward again. To see Ted suffer a *third* strike was an event four times more rare, and more remarkable, than seeing him get a hit. When Ted retired, attendance in the *league* dropped alarmingly. In Boston, where millions came through the years, to cheer, to boo, to care what he did, there was an accretion of memory so bright, bittersweet, and strong that when he left, the light was gone. And Fenway was left with a lesser game.

All hail the Kid! On April 9, 1969, Washington, D.C., Mayor Walter Washington presented the keys to the city to two kindred spirits: new Senators manager Ted Williams and new Redskins coach Vince Lombardi.Each had reached the pinnacle of his profession in another venue; each was viewed hopefully as the savior of a moribund team. Three years earlier there had come to Ted the greatest honor a ballplayer can attain: induction into the Baseball Hall of Fame. But perhaps the most moving tribute of all was the 1985 unveiling of Armand LaMontagne's wooden statue of the Kid in all his glory, at the bat. Louise Kaufman was with him for that.

Golf is the game of choice among baseball players in general, and retired players especially. For Ted golf was okay, but it wasn't as much fun as fishing, and hitting a golf ball sure as hell wasn't as hard as hitting a baseball. Ted's buddy Sam Snead, with whom he went into a fishing-tackle business in Florida, would say that you had to play your foul balls in golf and that a jumpy guy like Williams would never have made it on the pro circuit. Maybe. But Williams could play golf better than Snead could play baseball, and Snead was still a world-class golfer in his *sixties*.

around, the best is Ted." But soon there were scores of boats in the bay, and not so many fish. And even the Miramachi had no pools with salmon wall to wall. And Ted walked away from the tournaments. There wasn't the feeling of men together, or sport in them. Somehow, they'd changed. Or maybe it was Ted.

Last year, Ted and Lou went up to Cooperstown. This was for the unveiling of a statue of the Kid. There are many plaques in the Hall of Fame, but only two statues: just the Babe and him. And Ted went into the Hall this time, pulled the sheet off his statue, and looked at his young self in the finish of that perfect swing. He looked and he looked, while the crowd got quiet, and the strobes stopped flashing. And when he tried to speak, he wept.

Hey, where the hell is he?" It's after four, and Ted's getting hungry. "I'M GONNA CALL HIM."

Lou says: "Don't be ugly."

"I'm not ugly," Ted insists, but quietly. He dials and bends to look at me. "Hey, if this guy doesn't come, you can eat. You wanna eat here?" Then to the phone: "WHERE THE HELL ARE YOU?"

"Ted, don't be mean."

"I'm not. YEAH, TOMORROW? WELL, OKAY, BUDDY." Ted has had a successful phone conversation. Quick, and to the point.

"Awright, you can eat. Hey, Sweetie, take him up so he can see."

Now pitching for the Sears team … Ted Williams. Looking almost as silly and uncomfortable as Ted in this 1960 picture are, from the left, Sears bigwigs George Struthers, Crowdus Baker, and Charles Kellstadt.

There are no mementos in the living room, but Lou has put a few special things in a little room upstairs. Most of the pictures have to do with Ted, but the warmth of the room, and its character, have to do with Louise. This is no shrine. It is a room for right now, and a handsome little place, too. Now, it is filled with her quiet energy. "Here's Ted Williams when I met him," she says. "And if that isn't gorgeous, I'll eat my hat." And here's a photo of Lou in shorts, with a fly rod, looking fragile next to a tarpon she pulled from Florida Bay. She does not seem fragile now. She is spry and able. She has been with Ted ten years straight, as near as anybody will say, and that speaks volumes for her strength and agility. She is sometimes angry that people do not credit Ted with tenderness—"You don't know him," she says, and her voice has a surprising edge—but she also knows he will never show it. So here she shows a lonely young Ted with a little suitcase, going off to flight school. Here's Ted and Tom Yawkey, and look: Mr. Yawkey has pictures of Ted behind him, too. "Here he is in Korea," says Louise. "You know, when he landed that plane, the blood was pouring from his ears. I have to tell people that… because he's so loud. Big, too." Lou picks up a cushion off a window seat. There are pictures beneath. "See, he's done so many things…"

"Hey, you want a drink?" Ted is calling. "TED WILLIAMS IS GONNA HAVE A DRINK."

Soon he flops into his chair with a tumbler, and hands over a videotape. He wants it in the VCR. He says: "This is the most wonderful guy, hell of a guy. Bill Ziegler. I'm responsible for getting him into the majors…" That was when Ted came back in '69 to manage the Senators. Bill Ziegler was the trainer.

"So he had a son and he named him Ted Williams Ziegler. You're gonna see him now. IS IT IN? HEY, YOU LISTENING?" The tape shows Ziegler's sons batting. Ziegler sends the tapes for analysis. The soundtrack sends out a steady percussion: *thwack… thwack… thwack*. Both of these boys get wood on the ball, and Ted has the sound up. Now he talks over it: "I'm gonna show you the first tape; then I'm gonna ask you what's the difference. See this kid, I told him his hips, he's got to get them OPEN…"

From the kitchen, Lou protests: "Ted! Not now. Wait for me!"

"SEE?…" *thwack* "Ground ball. A little slow with his hands."

From Lou: "Okay, Okay, I don't know nothin'."

"HANDS THROUGH!" *thwack* "Center field, always to center, see where his hips are pointed? He's got to" *thwack* "OPEN 'EM UP…"

From Lou, coming in, wiping her hands as she watches: "He doesn't step into it like Ted Williams."

Ted pretends he doesn't hear. "Hips come through OPEN…"

"He doesn't bring his hands around like you do, honey."

"Yeah, he's got to, GROUND BALL! see, when I'M up…" and now Ted takes his stance in the living room. "I'm grindin'…" now his hands are working. "I got the hands cocked. *COCKED!*" and, here's the pitch. "*BAMMMM!*" says Ted, as he takes his cut and asks: "We got Bill Ziegler's number? WHERE'S HIS NUMBER?"

Ted is yelling on the phone in the kitchen, and Lou is in the living room, fitting her thoughts to small silences. "When Ted talks…" *thwack* "it's always right now…"

"BILL, I WANNA SEE HIM ON HIS FRONT FOOT MORE, AND THE HANDS QUICK, *QUICK*…"

"You know, the baseball players… It's not macho, they're just… athletes, just beautiful boys…"

Ted hangs up and throws himself onto his chair: "AWRIGHT, MAJOR LEAGUE! LET'S SET IT UP." That means dinner. Lou's cooking Chinese tonight. Ted's still watching Ziegler's kids. "Ground ball. You don't make history hittin' 'em on the ground, boys." Now he pulls away from the TV. "Sweetie," he sings playfully, "we got any sake-o?" Lou sings: "Not tonight-eo." Ted sings: "Well, where's the wine-o?"

Lou says grace while all hold hands. Then we set to food, and Ted is major league. "It's good, huh?" he says between mouthfuls. "Well, isn't it? HEY! Aren't you gonna finish that rice?"

He's finished fast and back in his chair. "We got any sweets?"

A little album on the coffee table has pictures from Christmas. John

Ring out the old, ring in the new. Carl Yastrzemski had big shoes to fill when he took over left field for Boston in 1961. In 1967, one year after this photo was taken, he did it, winning the American League triple crown. He is the last man to have done so, as Williams is the last to have hit .400. (The Kid also won the triple crown twice, in 1942 and 1947.)

Henry gave his letter of acceptance from Bates as his present to Ted. It's got Ted thinking about the car he's got to get, so John Henry can take a car to school. "Got to have a car…" He's thinking aloud so Louise can check this out. "Course, there's gonna have to be rules…" He's working it over in his mind, and he muses: "Maybe say that other than school… he can't take the car if his mother says no…" Lou is in a chair across the room. She's nodding. "HAVE to be rules," Ted says, "so he doesn't just slam out of the house… slam out and JUMP IN THE CAR…"

Something has turned in his gut, and his face is working, growing harder. There's a mean glitter in his eye, and he's thinking of his elder daughter, walking away from him…

"SLAM OUT… *LIKE MY DAUGHTER USED TO…*"

His teeth are clenched and the words are spat. It's like he's turned inside himself to face something we cannot see. It is a fearsome sight, this big man, forward, stiff in his chair, and hurling out ugly words at his vision of pain… I feel I should leave the room, but too late.

Out at home.

"…THAT BURNED ME…"

The switch is on. Lou calls it the Devil in him.

"…A PAIN IN MY HAIRY RECTUM!"

"Nice," says Lou. She is fighting for him. She has not flinched.

"Well, DID," he says through clenched teeth. "AND MAKES YOU HATE BROADS!…"

"Ted. Stop." But her Ted is gone.

"… HATE GOD!"

"TED!"

"…HATE LIFE!"

"TED!… JUST… STOP!"

"DON'T YOU TELL ME TO STOP. DON'T YOU *EVER* TELL ME TO STOP."

Lou's mouth twists up slightly, as she snorts: "HAH!"

And that does it. They have beaten it, or Lou has, or it's just gone away. Somehow, it's past, and Ted sinks back in his chair. His jaw is unclenched. He grins shyly. "You know, I love this girl, like I never…"

Lou sits back, too, and laughs.

"SHE'S IN TRAINING," Ted says. "I'M TEACHIN' HER…"

"He sure is," Lou says, like it's banter, but her voice is limp. She heads back to the kitchen, and Ted follows her with his eyes.

Then he finds me on his couch, and he's trying to sneer through his grin, as he yells: "WHEN ARE YOU LEAVING? HUH? BYE!

"JESUS, YOU'RE LIKE THE GODDAM RUSSIAN SECRET POLICE!"

"… OK, BYE! YEAH, SURE, GOOD-BYE!"

Ted walks me out to the driveway. As I start the car, Lou's face is a smile in the window, and Ted is bent at his belly, grabbing their Dalmatian puppy, tickling with his big hands while the dog rolls and paws the air. And as I ease the car into gear, I hear Ted's voice behind, cooing, very softly, now: "Do I love this little dog, huh?… Yes, this little shittin' dog… Yes, yes, I love you… Yes, I do."

Richard Ben Cramer, 1986

THE KID AT BAT

When Ted Williams first reported to the Red Sox spring training camp in 1938, as green a pea as ever came off the farm, his reputation preceded him. It wasn't his statistics that set him apart from mere mortals—in two years in the Pacific Coast League he posted modest batting averages of .271 and .291. It was The Swing. His first day in camp, when he stepped into the batting cage, everything stopped. Even the most veteran players interrupted their drills to watch the Kid strut his stuff: take the wide, erect stance that made him look even taller than his 6'3" height; extend his bat across the plate, as if taking its measure; wiggle his hips and rock his shoulders as if he were searching for solid ground beneath his feet; twist his hands on the bat handle with bad intent. Then, the turn of the hips, the snap of the wrists, the fluid follow-through, and the crack of bat on ball. No student of baseball who saw The Swing ever forgot it.

When Eddie Collins had come to San Diego in 1936 to check the progress of two Padres he had on option, Bobby Doerr and George Myatt, he spied this scrawny 17-year-old part-time pitcher taking batting practice, and he saw the most perfect batting form he had seen, better even than that of Joe Jackson. Collins talked Bill Lane, the Pads' owner, into a handshake deal for an option on the boy who had The Swing. One year later he came back to exercise the option, and Ted Williams became the property of the Boston Red Sox.

In later years many writers credited Collins with near-supernatural powers of prediction for staking his reputation on a kid who, to that point, had been to bat only once in the Pacific Coast League. But the old ivory hunter would merely say, "I just happened to be lucky enough to be there. Any good baseball man would have spotted him. Ted stood out on that field like a sore thumb."

"Because he is a 'pull hitter' some say he is actually pulling away from the ball at the instant of impact. The hip twist that seems to tilt back his trunk, combined with the popping of his wrists like a rattlesnake whip, is what creates this illusion. In baseball parlance he 'rides the ball.' Like the good golfer, he follows through with his weight."

—Al Wesson, 1942

THE KID IN SPRING

The Kid was born on August 30, 1918, to May Venzer Williams and Samuel Stewart Williams. Although the baseball record books list his formal handle as Theodore, the name on his birth certificate was Teddy Samuel Williams. If his parents were naming him in tribute to the rugged individualism of Teddy Roosevelt, they couldn't have been more prescient. The road to manhood for this Kid was long and dark, and if he was going to get there, he'd damned well have to find the way himself.

"My mother was gone all day and half the night, working the streets for the Salvation Army," Ted wrote in his autobiography. "I didn't see much of my dad…. My dad and I were never close. I was always closer to my mother, always feeling I had to do right by her, always feeling she was alone." *She* was alone? *He* had to do right by *her*? May Williams embraced the whole family of man through the Salvation Army; if that fervor for humanity left her husband and children—for Ted had a younger brother named Danny—a little short, well, they could trust to Providence as she did.

There is a story Ted tells about himself in another context—how bold and brash he was in 1938, his last year in the minors—that forms a paradigm for his progress through life. Late in a tie ballgame, he hit a double. Trying to distract the pitcher, he began to wave his arms and jitterbug off the base. Minneapolis Manager Donie Bush had seen him pull so many bonehead plays that he became nervous. "Don't go too far, now… be alert… watch that pitcher… look out for that pickoff!"

"Take it easy, Skip," the Kid yelled back. "I got here by myself, I'll get home by myself."

> "Ted is a wonderful son. He's never given me a moment's worry, and he's been a wonderful provider. He loves baseball just like I love my Salvation Army work."
>
> —May Williams, 1948

Ted's photographer father had a willing, happy subject in the six-year-old Ted, who was not the only one who posed for Sam Williams in a sailor suit. This was San Diego, a Navy town, and Sam's studio downtown was kept humming with sailors and their girls. The day would come when Ted would wear a Navy uniform again.

In 1946 John Chamberlain, in a profile in *Life*, wrote of May Williams that "growing up under her nervous but fascinating spell would either make or break any kid." Seemingly it made Ted (*pictured at the left*) and broke Danny, who rejected authority —parental and civil—as vigorously as Ted welcomed it. In significant ways, however, their upbringing splintered Ted, too. If the playground was his salvation, it was not a total substitute for home, any more than the evangelical army was for his mother (*pictured opposite with San Diego Mayor Harley Knox*). She and her husband split up in 1939, with Sam going north to the Bay Area. He had "stuck it out with my mother for twenty years," Ted wrote, "and finally he packed up, and I'd probably have done the same. My mother was a wonderful woman in many ways, but gee, I wouldn't have wanted to be married to a woman like that." Sam set up a photo shop in Oakland with his new wife, Minnie.

In the photo opposite, Ted's mom is the one in the simple cloth coat, not the one in furs. With her dedication to outfitting souls for the ascent to heaven, she couldn't be bothered much about everyday appearances. Second-hand furniture and clothing troubled her not a bit, for she ministered daily to those who had nothing. But Ted was ashamed of the shabbiness and neglect. "I was embarrassed about my home, embarrassed that I never had quite as good clothes as some of the kids, embarrassed that my mother was out in the middle of the damn street all the time." That shame inevitably transformed into rage, which had to find an outlet or, destructively, be turned inward. Sports became the answer for Ted, as it had for Ruth and Cobb and so many others; Danny never found an answer. In the team photo from Hoover High, 1935, sixteen-year-old Ted is at the lower left.

Ted's home had one undeniable plus: North Park playground was only a block and a half away, and its playing fields had lights. If his parents were going to be away from morning until night, at least Ted could play ball instead of sitting on the porch waiting for someone to come home. Roy Engle, Ted's fellow North Park regular who graduated from Hoover High a class ahead of him, said "We were kind of playground bums, I guess you'd say." Ted starred for the Padre Serra American Legion Post (he is in the back row, center), which was essentially the Hoover High team. After his graduation in 1936 he signed on with the fledgling San Diego Padres for $150 a month, as a pitcher-outfielder.

Frank Shellenback (*left*) was one of the greatest minor league pitchers ever, winning 295 games in the PCL. He was nearing the end of the trail as a pitcher in 1936 when he became the Padres' first manager—and Ted's. Just seventeen years old and playing in the top minor-league circuit in the country, he hit .271 in 42 games.

This was Ted in 1936, just after reporting to the hometown Padres, who the year before had been located in Hollywood. Ted had come close to signing with the Los Angeles Angels, but his dad, previously content to let Ted go his own way, now decided to get in on the act and scotched the deal. The Cardinals were the first big-league team to send a scout to look at him, but they didn't like the way he ran. The Yankees made an offer but wanted to start him way down the ladder. Detroit sent scout Marty Krug (*inset*), a former big-leaguer, who was aghast at Ted's beanpole frame, and passed him up. He told Ted's mother that a year of pro ball would literally kill him! It is surprising that someone in the Detroit front office did not literally kill Krug.

The public Ted Williams is a man of sharp contrasts to whom compromise and ambiguity are loathsome. This painting by Michael Schacht suggests the shades of gray that mark the private life.

Two views of a full house at Fenway in the 1940s. Ted beats out a rare infield hit, and Dom DiMaggio slides into third.

The Splendid Splinter may be a cloying, grating nickname, but you can see where it came from.

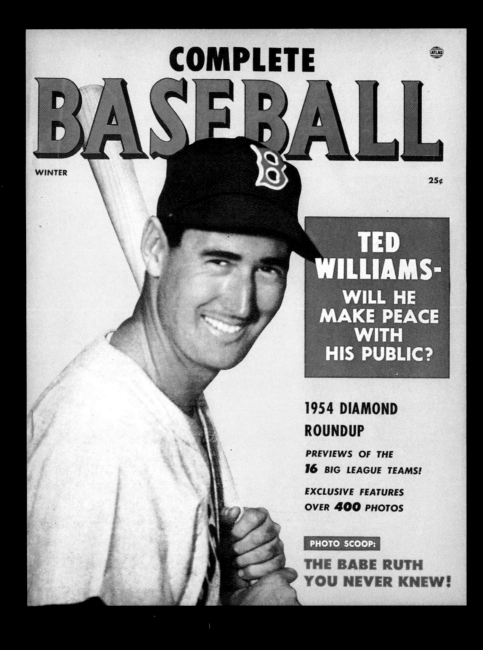

COMPLETE

BASEBALL

WINTER

25¢

TED WILLIAMS-

WILL HE MAKE PEACE WITH HIS PUBLIC?

1954 DIAMOND ROUNDUP

PREVIEWS OF THE **16** BIG LEAGUE TEAMS!

EXCLUSIVE FEATURES OVER **400** PHOTOS

PHOTO SCOOP:

THE BABE RUTH YOU NEVER KNEW!

The Kid as cover boy.

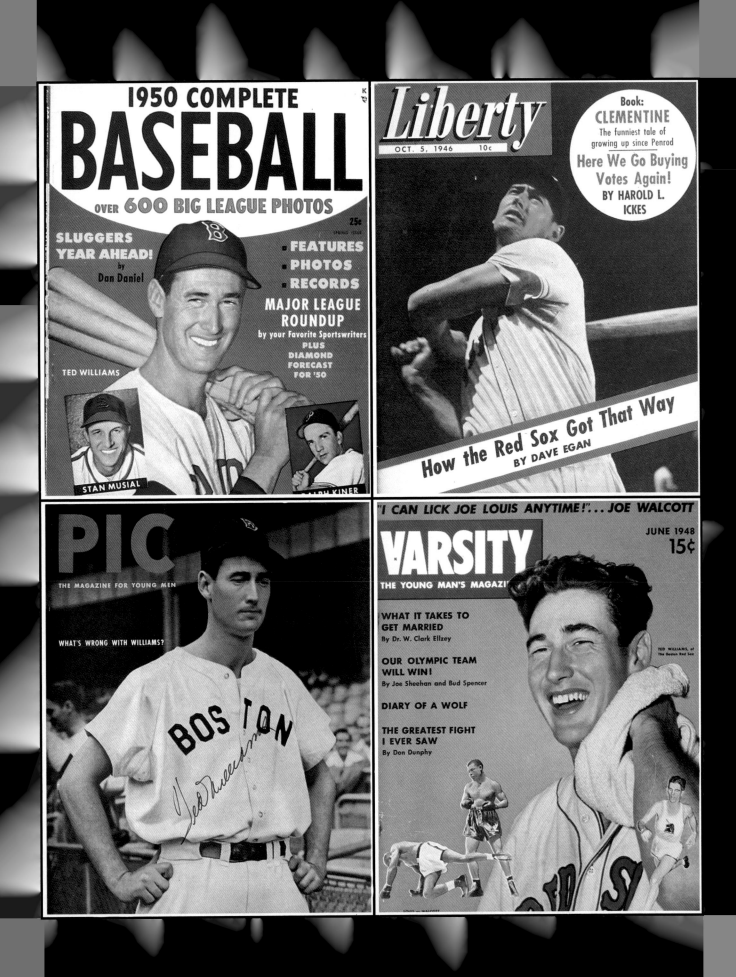

1950 COMPLETE BASEBALL

OVER **600** BIG LEAGUE PHOTOS

K

25¢
SPRING ISSUE

SLUGGERS YEAR AHEAD!
by Dan Daniel

- FEATURES
- PHOTOS
- RECORDS

MAJOR LEAGUE ROUNDUP
by your Favorite Sportswriters

PLUS
DIAMOND FORECAST FOR '50

TED WILLIAMS

STAN MUSIAL

RALPH KINER

Liberty

OCT. 5, 1946   10¢

Book: **CLEMENTINE**
The funniest tale of growing up since Penrod

Here We Go Buying Votes Again!
BY HAROLD L. ICKES

How the Red Sox Got That Way
BY DAVE EGAN

PIC

THE MAGAZINE FOR YOUNG MEN

WHAT'S WRONG WITH WILLIAMS?

BOSTON

Ted Williams

"I CAN LICK JOE LOUIS ANYTIME!"... JOE WALCOTT

VARSITY

THE YOUNG MAN'S MAGAZINE

JUNE 1948
15¢

WHAT IT TAKES TO GET MARRIED
By Dr. W. Clark Ellzey

OUR OLYMPIC TEAM WILL WIN!
By Joe Sheehan and Bud Spencer

DIARY OF A WOLF

THE GREATEST FIGHT I EVER SAW
By Don Dunphy

TED WILLIAMS, of The Boston Red Sox

LOUIS vs WALCOTT

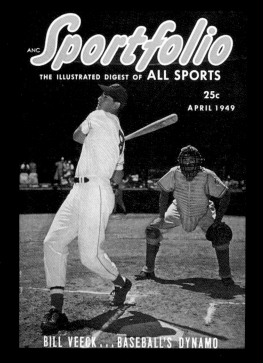

ANC *Sportfolio*
THE ILLUSTRATED DIGEST OF **ALL SPORTS**

25c
APRIL 1949

BILL VEECK...BASEBALL'S DYNAMO

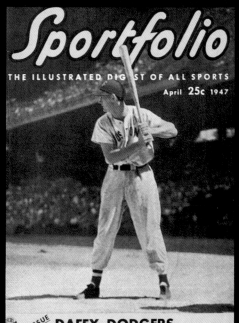

Sportfolio
THE ILLUSTRATED DIG ST OF ALL SPORTS

April 25c 1947

DAFFY DODGERS
Brooklyn's Old Laughing Gashouse Gang

"Eddie Collins used to say I lived
for my next turn at bat," Ted wrote
in his autobiography, "and that's
the way it was."

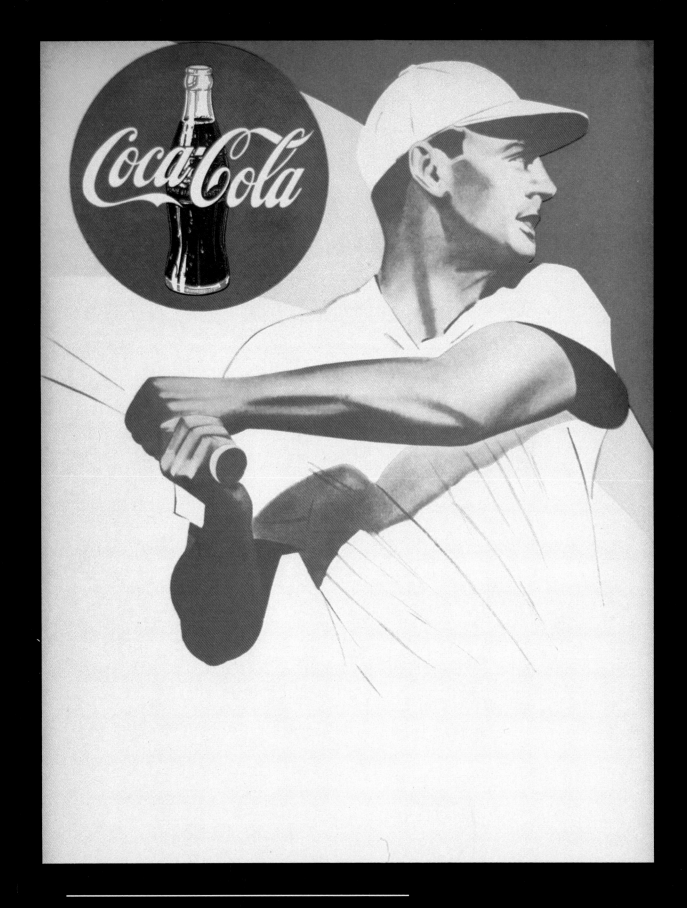

Ted promoted many products over the years, including a
competing soft drink, Moxie. Maybe that's why this rare
advertisement for Coca-Cola was never issued.

Two more shots of Ted with
the Padres in 1937, after two
years of methodically stuffing
himself with eggs, milk-
shakes, bananas, and ice
cream. He was still skinny,
but no longer ghastly.

On September 19, 1937 in the second half of a doubleheader in San Francisco that marked Ted's last game of the regular season, he provided a harbinger of things to come: he homered in his final at bat. In the seventh inning, with the wind whipping at his back, Missions' pitcher Wayne Osbourne said to his teammates, "If that guy thinks he can hit a homer against this gale he's gonna have to furnish his own power." Osbourne lobbed up a soft pitch (not unlike Rip Sewell's famous "eephus" pitch to Ted in the 1946 All Star Game). Ted ripped the ball through the gale, over the fence, across the street, and against a high wall 425 feet from home.

George Myatt (*left*) and Bobby Doerr were the two Padres under option to Boston in 1936. Late in that year Eddie Collins of the Bosox came out to San Diego. He declined to pick up the option on Myatt, who went on to play well for Washington in the war years, and replaced him with Ted Williams. Lane Field (*below*) was named for its owner, Bill Lane, who brought the Pacific Coast League to San Diego when it was a city of barely 100,000 people. (*Opposite*) The Swing was still the thing, but from 1937 to 1938 the uniform changed. Ted had been invited to Boston's spring camp in Sarasota, Florida, in 1938 but failed to win a spot. So it was off to Minneapolis, Nicollet Park, and a triple crown.

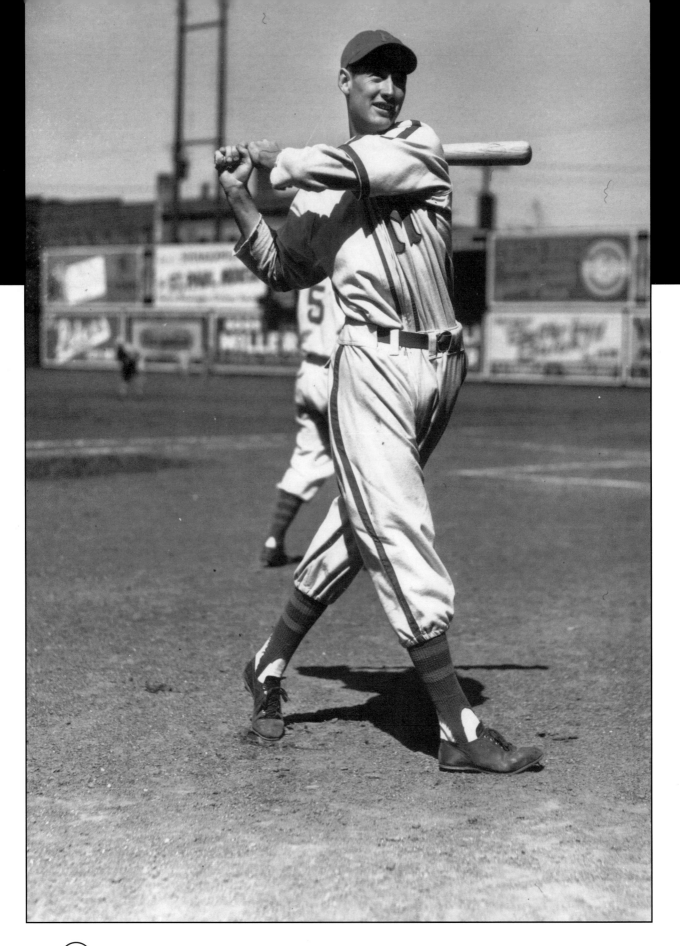

Ted had driven cross-country to Sarasota in 1938, talking hitting all the way with Bobby Doerr, a former teammate with the Padres who was to become an enduring friend. Babe Herman, a fading great, also was in the car; like Ted, he was trying to win a spot with the big club. Neither did, but Ted came away with the nickname that stuck for a lifetime: the Kid. Burning at his rejection by the Red Sox, he vented his frustration on American Association pitchers from Opening Day, when he made his debut in a Miller uniform with a homer, two singles, and four runs batted in.

The Kid was away from home for the first full year of his life, and mother and father were replaced by Minneapolis owner Mike Kelley and manager Donie Bush. "What a fiery kid he was," Kelley recalled in later years. "He gave Bush plenty of headaches. One day Donie came to me and said, 'Williams just popped out, then came into the dugout and broke the water cooler. [He punched it in, nearly slashing his wrist.] What should I do with him?' I told Donie to let Williams alone, that if he checked him up too short Williams' spirit would be broken." Kelley recognized what Bush did not—that Ted's greatness was inseparable from his intensity, was in fact a product of it, as it had been for Ty Cobb.

The Kid loved playing in cozy Nicollet Park, where Nick Cullop and Joe Hauser had become bush-league legends. But he was in a perpetual war with manager Donie Bush. One day he went out to right field (which he played all year in Minneapolis and his first year in Boston) without his sunglasses, and he lost a fly ball that brought home a couple of runs. Bush ran out to the outfield, screaming, "Where's your glasses? Where the *hell* are your glasses?" Ted replied matter-of-factly, "I forgot 'em, Skip." Bush was livid, but Ted couldn't figure out why he was so upset. Mike Kelley recalled, "Bush stormed into my office and said, 'I'll give that Williams just one more chance. If he pops off at me again I'll tell him to turn in his suit.' I said, 'When you do that, Donie, be sure that you and the rest of the players turn in your suits. Williams is my meal ticket.'" The next year, he would be Boston's.

Dec. 20c

BASEBALL
MAGAZINE

TED WILLIAMS, THE CENTENNIAL YEAR'S ACE ROOKIE

Four rookies made the team for Opening Day 1939. Excepting pilot Joe Cronin in the center, they are (*left to right*) Emerson Dickman, Williams, Jim Tabor (up from Minneapolis with Ted), and Woody Rich. Ted went on to a sensational freshman year, hitting .327 with 31 homers and a league-high 145 RBIs. After the season he did not return to San Diego, where his parents had just separated and his brother Danny was running with a bad crowd. "Home was never a happy place for me," Ted said, "and I had met a girl in Minnesota." The girl was Doris Soule, whom he would later marry. The next year, when the Kid incurred the antagonism of Boston writer Harold Kaese, he wrote, "Well, what do you expect from a guy who won't even go to see his mother in the offseason?" That same year Joe Miley of the *New York Post* wrote, "When it comes to arrogant and ungrateful athletes, this one leads the league." Ted never forgave them, not any of "them," and the long battle between the Kid and the Knights of the Keyboard was joined.

Jimmie Foxx (*below*) came up as a catcher and reached the big time at seventeen. In 1938 he hit 50 homers and drove in 175 runs for Boston, but he would never approach those figures again. He knew the Kid would be the banger to take over for him. (*Clockwise from the top of the opposite page*) Like Double X, the moody Lefty Grove had been a big part of the Philadelphia A's dynasty of 1929–31. His great fastball was only a memory by the time he came over to Boston, but he was incredibly effective at Fenway, supposedly a graveyard for lefthanders: over a three-year period his record there as a member of the Red Sox was 18–0. Doc Cramer was yet another Connie Mack alumnus, and played a fine center field until Dom DiMaggio made him expendable. Ben Chapman hit .340 for Boston in 1938; his reward was to be traded away to make room for Ted. Joe Vosmik, a career .307 hitter, was the left fielder in 1939; Ted moved over from right to take his place in 1940.

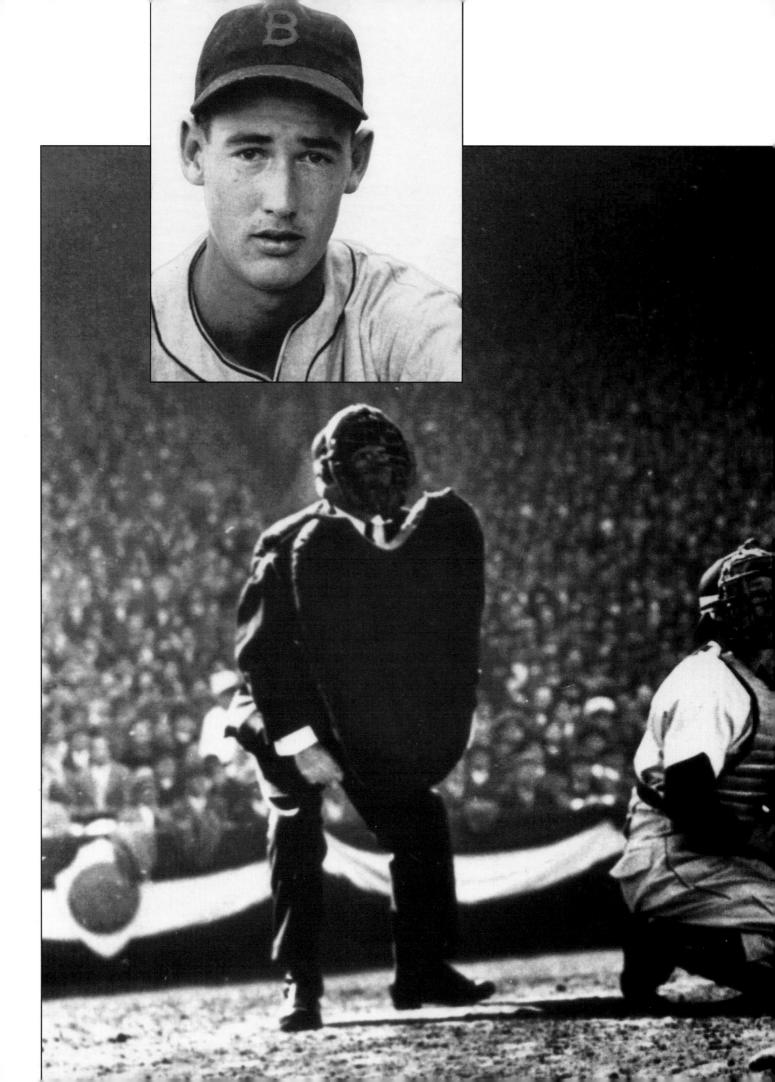

The Kid of 1939–42 was a marvel to behold: the awkwardness of a colt combined with the power of a Derby winner.

Jimmie Foxx (*top*) and Joe Cronin (*below*) followed Ted in the batting order in 1939 and '40. Both were veterans who led by example; shortstop Cronin, of course, was the player-manager. Ted had the highest regard for Joe as a player and as a man, but when the requisites of celebrity became excruciating for him in 1940–42, he wished that Joe would have stepped in on his behalf. "When I was a young player," Ted has written, "I needed and should have had some protection, some common meeting ground to head these things off before they got worse, which they always did." He was speaking in particular of his relations with the press and Cronin's failure to advise or shield him, but he might as well have been speaking about his own father's failure as a mentor.

(*Overleaf*) On August 24, 1940, the Tigers were marching to a pennant and were clobbering the Red Sox through seven innings. Boston's pitching staff had become depleted through the dog days of summer and Joe Cronin was looking for volunteers to mop up. The Kid, recalling his exploits at Hoover High and his one mercifully brief outing in the PCL in 1936, heard himself say, "Me. I'll pitch." And so he did, going two innings, allowing three hits and one run and, to his everlasting satisfaction, fanning slugger Rudy York on a sidearm curve.

(*Opposite*) Teammates surround Williams after he collided with Doc Cramer going for a liner in a game at Cleveland on June 24, 1940. After the incident, Ted spent the night in the hospital. Despite occasional lapses of concentration. Ted was, public perception today to the contrary, a better-than-average outfielder throughout the decade. He had a fine arm and covered a lot of ground. (*Below*) The Kid as a spectator at Cleveland in July of the following year. Pass the Wild-Root Cream Oil, Charlie.

Ted's three-run homer off Claude Passeau with two outs in the bottom of the ninth has just given the A.L. a 7–5 victory in the 1941 All Star Game. In the clubhouse afterward he shared his exhilaration with A.L. President Will Harridge and Yankee rival Joe DiMaggio.

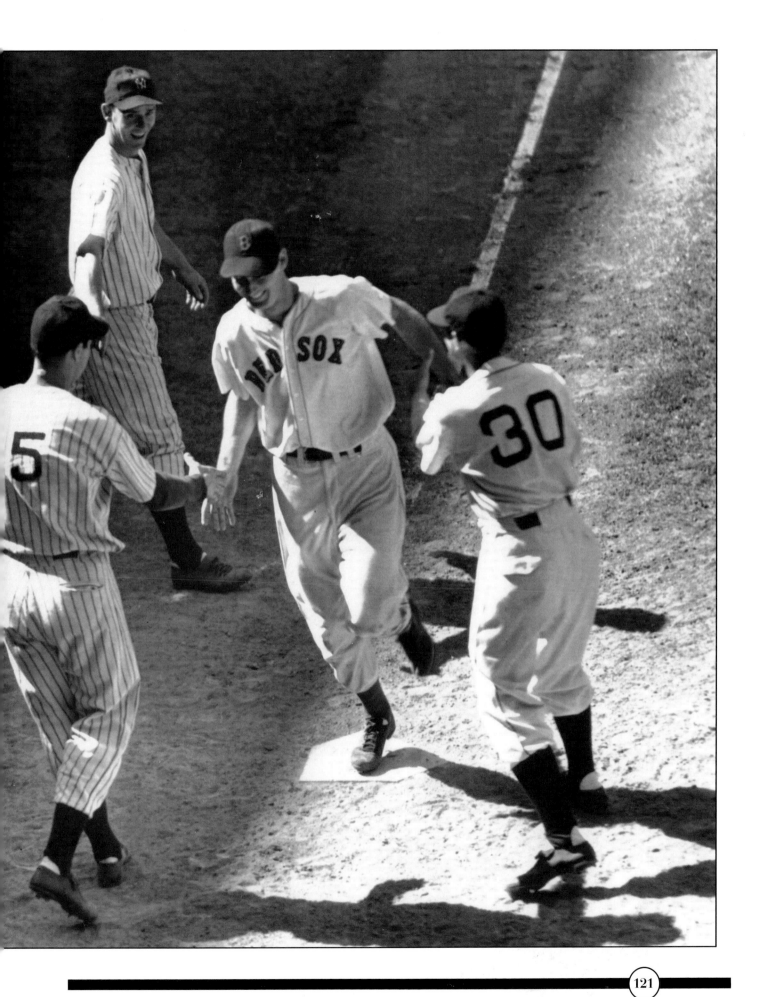

(*Below*) The Kid was always larger than life in Boston. (*Right*) Even though Joe D. won the 1941 MVP, Ted could console himself with *The Sporting News* award as Major League Player of the Year. That's publisher J. G. Taylor Spink at the far left. (*Opposite*) Coming back to play in 1942, Ted was still just one of the guys, but trouble was brewing over his III-A draft deferment.

Johnny Pesky (*above, left*) joined the Red Sox as a rookie in 1942 and batted .331 while leading the league in hits with 205. With future Hall of Famer Bobby Doerr he formed a first-rate keystone combo for several years. Doerr was Ted's best friend on the club. "I always envied Bobby the father he had," Ted said, "a father who was close to him, telling him what to do, encouraging him, helping him with his finances." The Kid never felt more alone and in need of someone in his corner than in the spring of '42, when fans and writers unfeelingly questioned his courage, his integrity, and his patriotism. Not helping his image were publicity shots like the one of him playing cricket with Britain's Royal Air Force cadets at the Lakeland, Florida, School of Aeronautics.

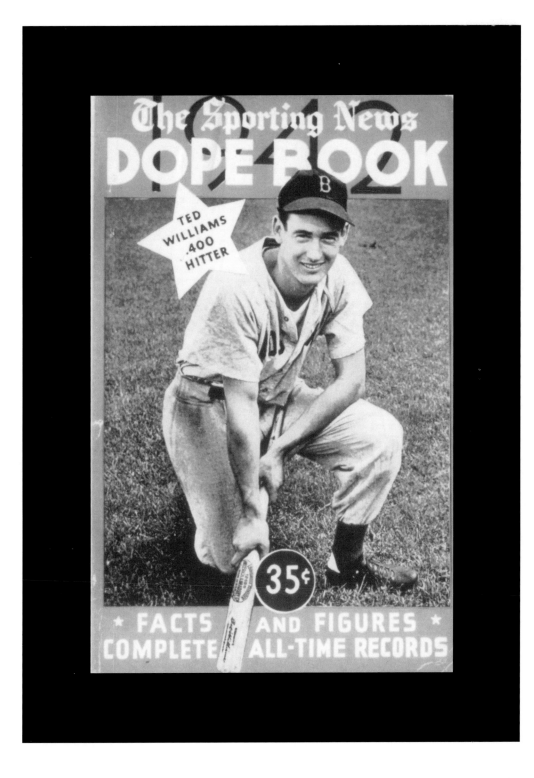

THE KID IN SUMMER

What Ted Williams accomplished in 1941 was the stuff of legend, especially his remarkable final-day performance that cleared the .400 hurdle. But the Kid was not extracting much joy from the public's acclaim, not the way he had in 1939, when he was the toast of the town and tipped his cap flamboyantly to the crowd after any good-sized cheer.

He had begun to sense in 1940, with the public discussion over his offseason travel plans, that the lot of the baseball star was not a happy one: to pass from Novice to Hero to Celebrity to Commodity to Trash. When the left-field faithful at Fenway booed him one day after he dropped a fly ball and then struck out, it occurred to Ted that admirers who were that fickle maybe weren't worth courting; he resolved then and there never to tip his hat to the crowd again.

Then came the draft-deferment ruckus of 1942 and the Kid, who was being acclaimed as the greatest hitter since Ruth, withdrew further into the safety of his self. His dedication to his craft still burned as brightly as ever; unparalleled glory lay ahead. His way with the fans, however, was not destined to be that of Ruth but instead the path blazed by Cobb, Hornsby, and Terry—individualists whose dedication, concentration, and intensity led them above others who may have had equal natural gifts. Like Charles Lindbergh, the Lone Eagle who had been Ted's boyhood hero, these men had a disregard for public opinion and a combative, self-protective streak. These men also had, unlike Ruth, a perpetual war with the press.

The summer of Ted Williams' life would be long and hot, and too often its fruits would be bitter.

> **"I always admired Charles Lindbergh, the hero that he was, the terrible tragedy he had to live with, his great obsession to be alone despite the important things he did, to keep his life free from the limelight."**
>
> —*Ted Williams, 1969*

(*Top*) Ted retrieves a
bat he had flung at a
pigeon, 1942. (*Left*)
Full house at Fenway,
a boo-bird's view.

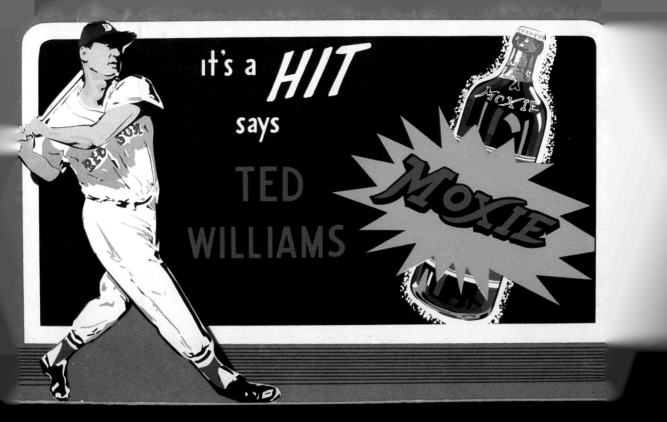

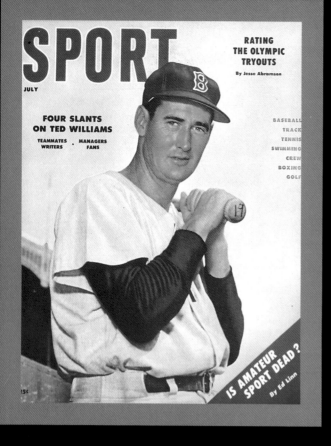

SPORT

JULY

RATING
THE OLYMPIC
TRYOUTS
By Jesse Abramson

FOUR SLANTS
ON TED WILLIAMS
TEAMMATES · MANAGERS
WRITERS · FANS

BASEBALL
TRACK
TENNIS
SWIMMING
CREW
BOXING
GOLF

IS AMATEUR
SPORT DEAD?
By Ed Linn

25¢

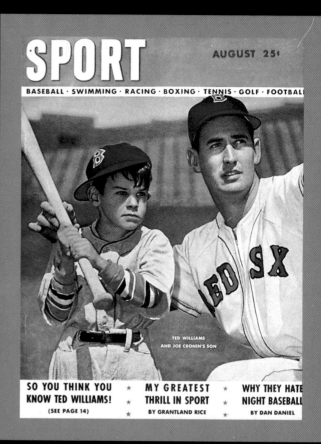

SPORT   AUGUST 25¢

BASEBALL · SWIMMING · RACING · BOXING · TENNIS · GOLF · FOOTBALL

TED WILLIAMS
AND JOE CRONIN'S SON

SO YOU THINK YOU   MY GREATEST   WHY THEY HATE
KNOW TED WILLIAMS!   THRILL IN SPORT NIGHT BASEBALL
(SEE PAGE 14)   BY GRANTLAND RICE BY DAN DANIEL

Although *Sport* ran some of
the most glorious color
photographs of the Kid ever
produced, it was his least
favorite magazine. For six
years from the time it
overstepped his bounds of
propriety and printed a
discussion with his mother in
1948, Ted wouldn't speak
with any of its writers. To the
end of his playing days,
anyone affiliated with *Sport*
found him a most daunting
subject for interview.

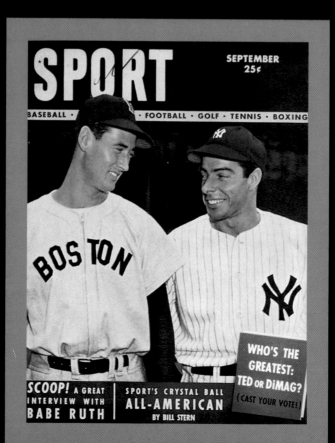

SPORT   SEPTEMBER
                      25¢

BASEBALL · · FOOTBALL · GOLF · TENNIS · BOXING

BOSTON

NY

SCOOP! A GREAT
INTERVIEW WITH
BABE RUTH

SPORT'S CRYSTAL BALL
ALL-AMERICAN
BY BILL STERN

WHO'S THE
GREATEST:
TED OR DiMAG?
(CAST YOUR VOTE!)

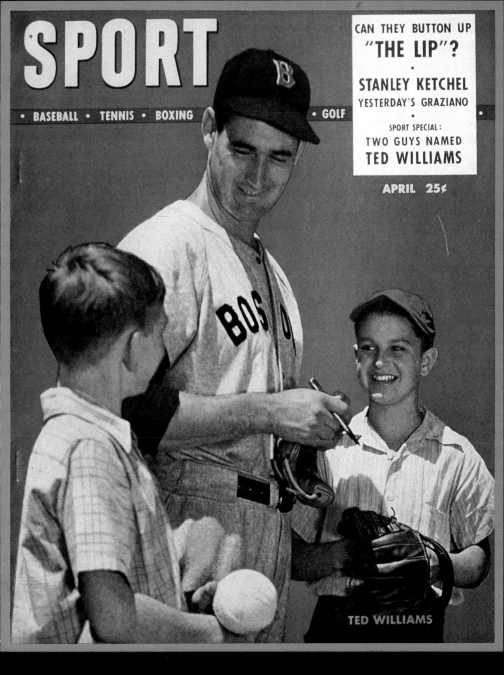

SPORT

CAN THEY BUTTON UP
"THE LIP"?
·
STANLEY KETCHEL
YESTERDAY'S GRAZIANO
·
SPORT SPECIAL:
TWO GUYS NAMED
TED WILLIAMS

APRIL 25¢

BOSTON

TED WILLIAMS

Posing Ted with children was a sure shot. His empathy with them was extraordinary: he never lost touch with what it felt like to be a kid, and he gave abundantly what he himself had so keenly missed, friendship and guidance.

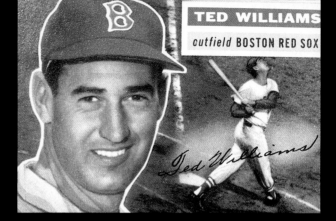

TED WILLIAMS outfield BOSTON RED SOX

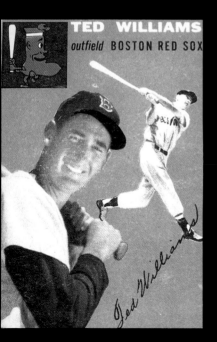

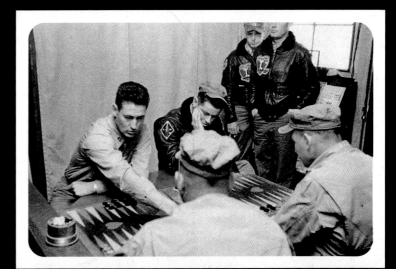

The Kid in Korea: five shots
from the July 18, 1953 issue
of *Collier's*.

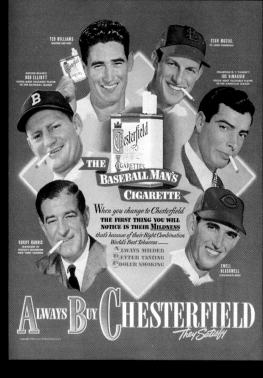

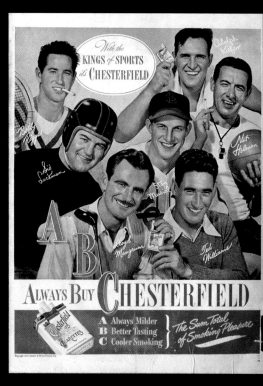

The Boston Sunday *Globe-Traveler* magazine of
March 27, 1960 paired Williams with other future
Hall of Famers in the twilight of their careers:
Early Wynn, Stan Musial, and Warren Spahn.

This splendid photo by Ozzie Sweet
ran in the the July 1956 issue of *Sport*.

Ted's fielding was largely untutored, but he never tired of talk about hitting; here he picks up pointers from Paul Waner.

After winning his III-A deferment on appeal to the Presidential Board, and rejecting the opinions of elders like Tom Yawkey and Mickey Cochrane that he shouldn't play in 1942, in May Williams signed up for service *his* way. By November he was in preliminary ground school at Amherst College, applying himself in the classroom as he seldom did at Hoover High.

"GETTING IN SHAPE FOR BASEBALL SHOULD BE EASY— PLAN TO WEAR GI SHOES ALL THROUGH THE TRAINING PERIOD."

-THIS YEAR TED HAS FORSAKEN BASEBALL FOR FISHING!

-FIGURE I HAVE AT LEAST THREE OR FOUR GOOD YEARS LEFT IN WHICH I SHOULD HIT AROUND 400"

-WHEN TED DID PLAY- HE HADN'T LOST ANY OF HIS BATTING POWER.
-HIT ONE BALL ON BRONSON FIELD THAT THEY SAY LANDED IN THE NEXT COUNTY!

"AFTER BASEBALL, I'M GOING TO BE A SPORTING GOODS SALESMAN. MY KNOWLEDGE OF GUNS AND SPORTS SHOULD BE A BIG ASSET IN SELLING!"

AS TOLD TO BOB COYNE BY LIEUT. ALEX WELCH U.S.N

TED WILLIAMS
..SOCIAL LIFE IN THE SERVICE DIDN'T APPEAL TO HIM - NEVER PURCHASED A SET OF WHITES!

From Amherst Ted went to preflight training at Chapel Hill, North Carolina; then flight training at Kokomo, Indiana; from there to the U.S. Naval Air Station at Pensacola, Florida, for advanced flight training as a Marine Corps pilot. (It was at Pensacola that he married Doris Soule and, more enduringly, learned to love Florida's fishing.) Next, over to Jacksonville for operational combat training. Ted finally received his orders and made it all the way to Honolulu as the War ended.

Lieutenant and flight instructor Williams looks pretty glum in this scene at the Pensacola Station's coffee bar, but he really liked the military life. Under the discipline and order that other men might have found oppressive, he felt somehow more free than ever before.

Like all major leaguers in the service, Ted played some baseball, but his heart wasn't really in it: in his own estimation, "I played lousy." (*Left*) Cadet Williams poses with Lientenant George D. Kepler, head baseball coach at the Chapel Hill preflight school. (*Below left*) The thrill of anticipation is evident on his face as Ted sits in the rear cockpit of the N2S trainer and listens to his flight instructor.

Four former major leaguers were on the Bronson Field team at Pensacola: (*left to right*) Bob Kennedy of the Chicago White Sox, Nick Tremark of the Brooklyn Dodgers, Ray Stoviak of the Philadelphia Phillies, and the Kid. Of the four, Williams had the lowest batting average.

WHO'S WHO in BASEBALL

1943
TWENTY-EIGHTH
EDITION

TED
WILLIAMS

PRICE
25c

By the time the 1943 issue of *Who's Who in Baseball* hit the stands, cover boy Ted was out of baseball. He came back to Boston on July 12, 1943, to take part in a city-sponsored game. He met Babe Ruth for the first time, and reconnected with Doris, then his fiancée and residing in Beantown. After the game, it was back to wartime duties.

Whether sparring in the Navy (with Chapel Hill boxing coach Alfred Wolff) or with the press (trading barbs with Red Barber), fishing the Gulf of Mexico or hunting in the plains of Nebraska, Ted studied, prepared himself for the opposition, and gave the match all he had.

Ted is overbearingly the teacher—hitting, fishing, flying, photography, affairs of state, you name it—and that is because he is ever the student, insatiably curious and never satisfied. Even after he had a .406 season under his belt, he solicited batting advice from worthy veterans like Hugh Duffy (who had set the record of .438 back in 1894). But if batting tips from peers were welcome, intrusions by autograph solicitors were not.

Before the War, Ted was impetuous, unable to deal with frustration. He blew up, threw things, raged out of control. With maturity came a measure of outer restraint, but his gut still churned. "In a crowd of cheers," he wrote, "I could always pick out the solitary boo." Ted and Joe DiMaggio (posed above with Dom) competed for the public's affection while disavowing any concern with it, but they were truly brothers under the skin— both of them hypersensitive, distrustful, and perfectionist. After the War, Ted's return to a Red Sox uniform was typically heroic (*above, right*), driving a home run into the bleachers on Opening Day in the nation's capital. The Fenway fans of 1946 adored him and Ted reciprocated, good-naturedly participating in wacky promotions. The Red Sox cruised through spring and summer and all was right with the world, until the fall.

(*Overleaf*) Ted with his peers. By almost every statistical measure, the Babe takes first place and the Kid comes in second. But if Ted hadn't lost nearly five years in the military, the stats would tell a different story. Joe DiMaggio was a better outfielder and superior baserunner. But his hallmark achievement, hitting in 56 straight games in 1941, was matched by Ted's batting .406. Even over the span of Joe's streak, however, Ted hit for a higher average.

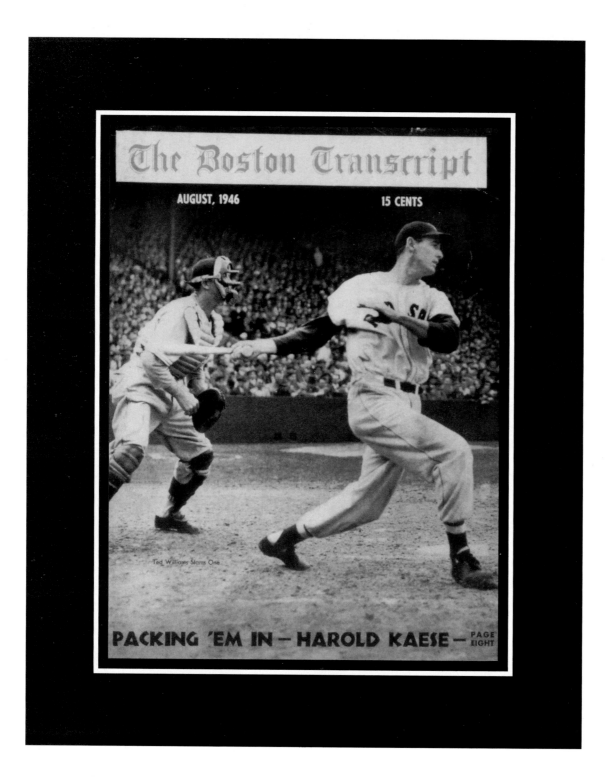

The Boston Transcript

AUGUST, 1946   15 CENTS

Ted Williams Slams One

PACKING 'EM IN — HAROLD KAESE — PAGE EIGHT

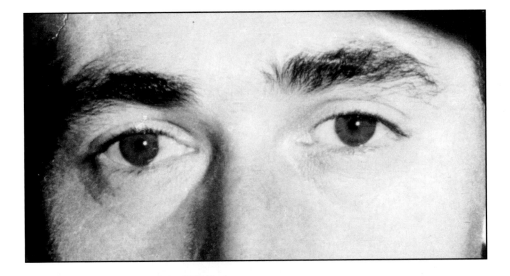

In the art of hitting a baseball, eyes and hands are nothing compared to head and heart. "A lot of people have 20–10 vision," Ted once wrote. "The reason I saw things was that I was so intense." His concentration and confidence, his perseverance and plan—these seem to emanate from Michael Schacht's painting.

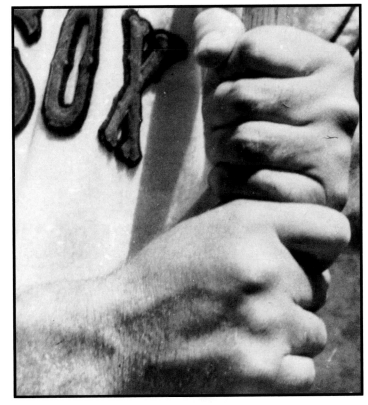

During the 1946 World Series, when the Red Sox squared off against the Cardinals, St. Louis manager Eddie Dyer employed a modification of the Boudreau Shift against Williams. In a pregame skull session, Ted and Joe Cronin reviewed their options.

151

When Ted posed with Bobby Doerr
and Rudy York for the cover of
Baseball Magazine, the Red Sox
were assured of the pennant, but in
September they lost six straight
games and, in a locker-room
confrontation, York accused Ted of
loafing. Finally, on September 13
in Cleveland, the Sox clinched the
flag, winning 1–0 as Ted crossed
up Lou Boudreau's Shift and
recorded an inside-the-park home
run, the only one of his career. Ted
missed the team party afterward,
preferring to tie flies with a local
fishing expert. What should have
been the happiest time of Ted's
career was rapidly turning sour,
and in the World Series it curdled:
St. Louis held Ted to only five hits,
all singles, and won the title.
Opposite, a Gene Mack cartoon
story of Game 1, in which York was
the hero. *Below*, the Dyer Defense
in action in Game 2.

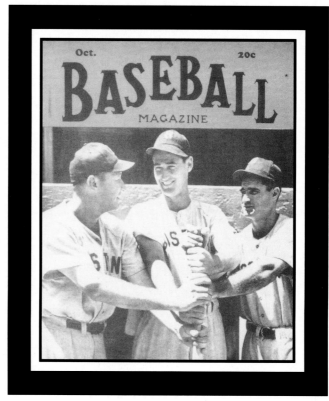

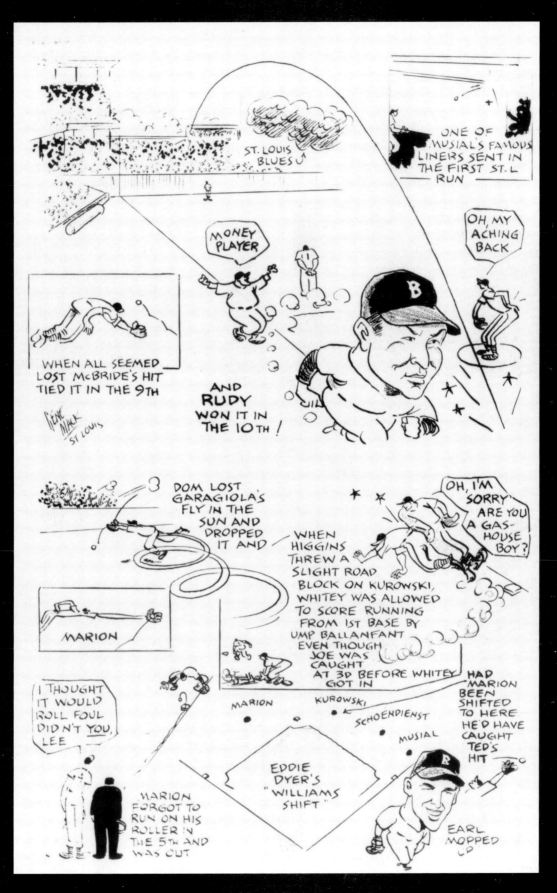

(*Above*) Ted is out at second as Red Schoendienst completes the double play in Game Six. (*Right*) Enos Slaughter scores the winning run in the final game as Johnny Pesky holds the relay throw. (*Opposite*) Ted, who popped out in the top of the eighth with the lead run on third, sits dejectedly at his locker. That's pitcher Mickey Harris with him. The Kid would never get a chance to redeem himself in another World Series.

Ted's precision when it came to selecting and caring for his bats was legendary. He would "bone" the entire length of the bat to tighten the grain and strengthen the wood. He would apply pine tar to the handle but would wipe it off with alcohol after every game to prevent rot. He ordered his bats to be 33 ounces, and if one of a batch was off by half an ounce, he could detect it. And when he was young, Ted would take his bats to the post office to weigh them, to make sure that they had not gained weight through absorption of moisture in the air. (*Above*) Ted inspects the efforts of a bat turner with catcher Buddy Rosar.

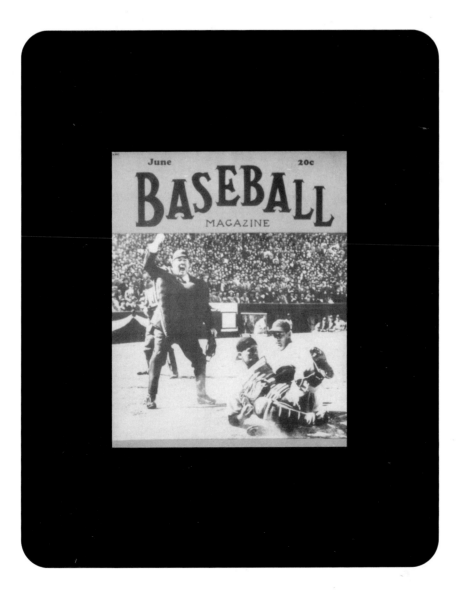

Ted could be telling Eddie Collins and Joe Cronin a whopper about the one that got away, or he could be talking about the contract he just landed for 1947, estimated at the time as $70,000. Ted gave fair return for his money in. He won his second triple crown and his third *Sporting News* Player of the Year Award, but in the MVP balloting he came up one point short of Joe DiMaggio. Boston writer Mel Webb left Ted off his ballot entirely; even a tenth-place nod would have given Ted the Award. Why did he do it? "I don't like the sonofabitch," he told one press colleague, "and I'll *never* vote for him!" (*Opposite, bottom*) Ted and Doris, who on January 28, 1948, became parents.

Joe McCarthy, long-time Yankee pilot, emerged from retirement to take the helm of the Red Sox. When a newsman asked if he thought he would have any trouble with Williams, McCarthy replied: "Any manager who can't get along with a .400 hitter ought to have his head examined."

(*Below*) Ted goes from first to third on a single in a stretch victory over the Yankees in 1948. McCarthy led the Red Sox to a tie for the 1948 pennant. In a one-game playoff with Cleveland, however, the Red Sox fell to pitcher Gene Bearden and shortstop Lou Boudreau. Next year, "Marse Joe" brought the Bosox into a final two-game series against his old club with a one-game lead; alas for Boston fans, the Yanks swept their way to the flag. Williams always called McCarthy the best manager he ever played for.

Ted's two hits contributed to a 2–1 American League win in the 1947 All Star Game at Wrigley Field. A.L. President Will Harridge shows his appreciation. Williams never forgot that Harridge had publicly stood up for him in the draft ruckus of 1942, when even Tom Yawkey advised him to bow to the hecklers. (*Below*) Ted squares off against Bob Feller, the great hurler of the decade, who like him had lost prime years to military service.

Ted Williams' first rule of hitting was: Get a good ball to hit. By that he meant not simply a pitch in the strike zone but one in the *hitter's* zone, as indicated by the higher batting averages in this now-celebrated schematic, first run in *Sports Illustrated*.

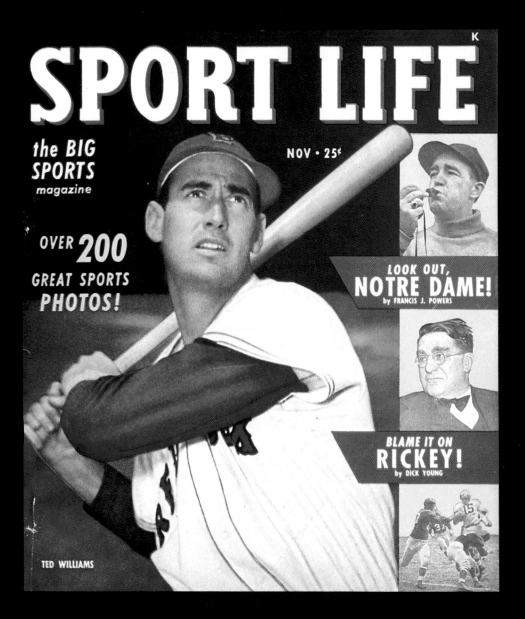

SPORT LIFE

the BIG SPORTS magazine

NOV · 25¢

OVER 200 GREAT SPORTS PHOTOS!

LOOK OUT, NOTRE DAME! by FRANCIS J. POWERS

BLAME IT ON RICKEY! by DICK YOUNG

TED WILLIAMS

Sport periodicals came and went, but the Kid stayed on, gracing cover after cover.

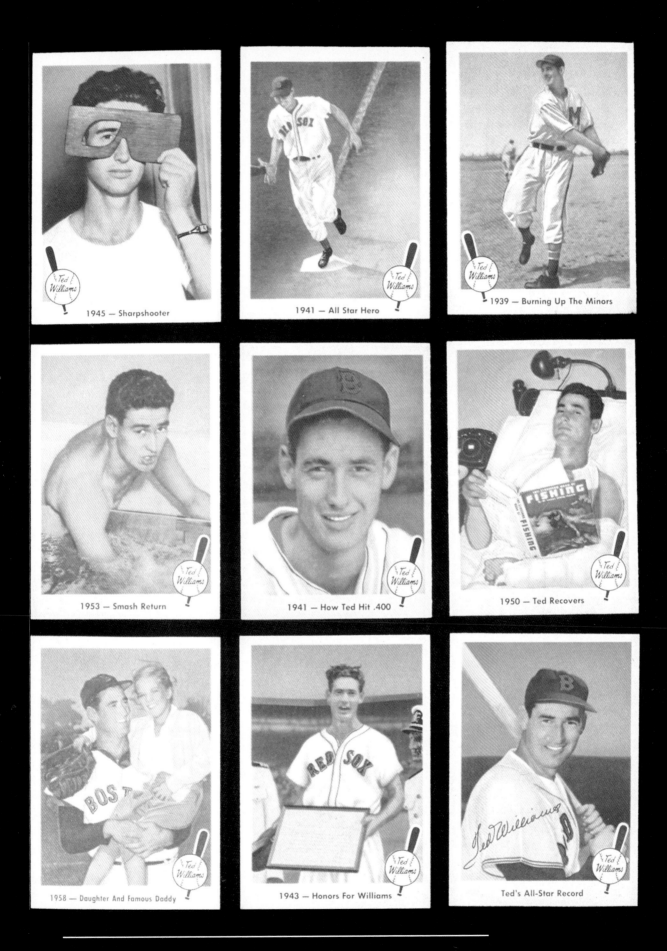

1945 — Sharpshooter

1941 — All Star Hero

1939 — Burning Up The Minors

1953 — Smash Return

1941 — How Ted Hit .400

1950 — Ted Recovers

1958 — Daughter And Famous Daddy

1943 — Honors For Williams

Ted's All-Star Record

In 1959 the Fleer confection company of Philadelphia issued its first baseball card set, an 80-card portrait of Ted Williams.

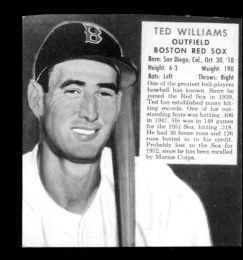

TED WILLIAMS
OUTFIELD
BOSTON RED SOX
Born: San Diego, Cal., Oct. 30, '18
Height: 6-3   Weight: 190
Bats: Left   Throws: Right
One of the greatest ball-players
baseball has known. Since he
joined the Red Sox in 1939,
Ted has established many hitting records. One of his out-
standing feats was batting .406
in 1941. He was in 148 games
for the 1951 Sox, hitting .318.
He had 30 home runs and 126
runs batted in to his credit.
Probably lost to the Sox for
1952, since he has been recalled
by Marine Corps.

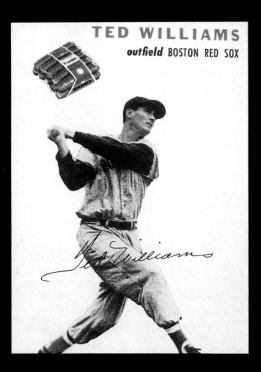

TED WILLIAMS
outfield BOSTON RED SOX

TED WILLIAMS
OUTFIELD, BOSTON RED SOX

TED WILLIAMS

(*Opposite*) A miscellany of early 1950s cards, with Ted's image selling everything from Leaf gum and Red Man chewing tobacco to Wilson Wieners and Wheaties. (*This page*) The Kid against the Crowd; two from *Collier's*, 1946.

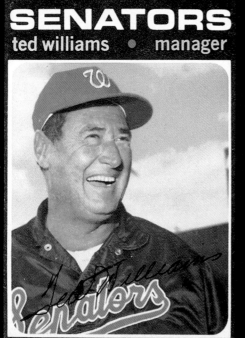

SENATORS
ted williams • manager

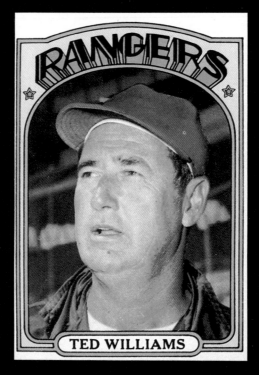

RANGERS

TED WILLIAMS

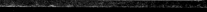

More commercialization of the Kid: Topps bubble gum in the early 1970s, Post Sugar Crisp and Havoline Motor Oil in the 1950s, and a clearly unauthorized use of his likeness on a condom pack in the 1940s.

CHAMP
PROPHYLACTICS

BASEBALL'S GREAT TED WILLIAMS SAYS

"**KIDS** GET THESE
MAJOR LEAGUE PATCHES **FREE**"

You'll find a colorful, sturdy cloth baseball patch in every special giant Sugar Crisp box. Each patch is 3 inches big! No sewing—just stick them on bikes, books, walls, clothing! Get Sugar Crisp and get going on your collection.

ONE PATCH IN EVERY SPECIAL GIANT SUGAR CRISP BOX

A Star is Made, not Born

Baseball's famed Ted Williams has three rules for any hitter who wants to go from good to great: *practice, practice* and *practice*. Nature can provide talent but needs help to make a great batting star — and help in making a great motor oil like *Advanced Custom-Made Havoline*.

Ted Williams is a member of the Advisory Staff of Champions of The Wilson Sporting Goods Co.

...and the Best motor oil is <u>Made</u>, not Born

Wear-proofs your engine for the life of your car

Advanced CUSTOM-MADE

HAVOLINE MOTOR OIL

EXTRA HEAVY DUTY

TEXACO

THE TEXAS COMPANY

The best oil nature can offer — *oil alone* — just doesn't have what it takes to keep modern engines out of trouble.

For these new motors it was obvious, in test after test, that a better oil had to be *built*. For today's toughest lubricating job — your new engine — Texaco engineers made *Advanced Custom-Made Havoline*.

Here is the best motor oil superior refining can produce, *made better* by a Balanced-Additive formula. A *tougher* motor oil, so advanced in anti-wear qualities that it actually *wear-proofs your engine for the life of your car*.

It keeps your engine clean, free from harmful sludge, rust and bearing-eating acids — and because it keeps your engine clean, you get the utmost in gasoline economy. Get Havoline at your Texaco Dealer's — *the best friend your car has ever had.*

TEXACO DEALERS... IN ALL 48 STATES

Texaco Products are also distributed in Canada and in Latin America

Where the Kid was "discovered" in 1936, San Diego's Hoover High playing field, still in use.

Ted with Smokey Joe Wood, the .406 of 1941 immortalizing one, the 34–5 in 1912 (plus three World Series wins) the other.

In the cauldron of the ballpark or the cool of the bay, the battle rages on.

Stan "the Man" Musial was the terror of the National League year after year, but never so much as in 1948, when he hit .376. Ted "the Kid" Williams scarcely trailed him, at .369.

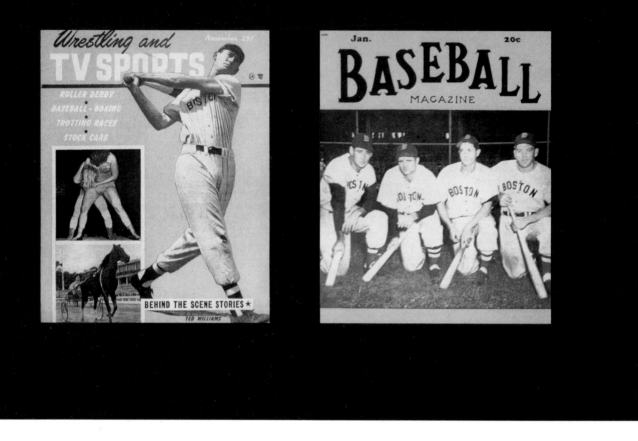

Those who anticipated difficulties for Ted with Joe McCarthy's strict curfews and no-nonsense approach ignored the Kid's history. He had never had any real trouble dealing with authority—managers, umpires, military superiors—perhaps because when he was a boy right and wrong were dogmatically defined in his home. He had boundless admiration for figures of authority in baseball like Connie Mack (shown opposite with Ted and pitcher Boo Ferriss), who exuded confidence and rectitude. He respected the old man's *fairness*: on the final day of the 1946 season, he instructed his pitchers to go after the .400 hitter, neither laying the ball in nor avoiding the plate. It was the *unfairness* of the fans and, especially, the press that Ted couldn't abide, that so deeply wounded him: "I wasn't a 'team' man. I was 'jealous.' I 'alienated' the players from the press. I didn't hit to left field. I took too many bases on balls. I did this, I did that. And so on. And so unfair." Ted cited as an example his unappreciated peace-maker role in a melee that broke out during the 1948 preseason exhibition between the Braves and Red Sox at Braves Field. Earl Torgeson of the Braves and Billy Hitchcock of the Red Sox were duking it out when Ted jumped on Torgeson and pinned him while others pulled Hitchcock away. Afterwards, the writers' first question to Torgeson was, "Did Williams hit you while you were down?" (*Above*) The quartet of Red Sox sluggers on the cover of the January 1949 issue of *Baseball Magazine* are, left to right, Ted, Bobby Doerr, Dom DiMaggio, and Vern Stephens.

(*Opposite*) The uniform numbers of Doerr, Williams, Cronin, and Pesky's predicted a pennant for 1946 but not, seemingly, a Series win. With McCarthy replacing Cronin at the helm for 1948–49 and new blood coming in—southpaw Mel Parnell (*far left*) and former Browns Vern "Junior" Stephens and Jack Kramer—prospects looked rosy again, but the results were if anything more disappointing. Even Detroit veteran Birdie Tebbets became an All-Star backstop in his new uniform. (*This page*) Johnny Pesky's acrobatics shifted from shortstop to third to accommodate newcomer Stephens, who batted cleanup behind the Kid; in 1949 *each* drove in 159 runs, an individual level not reached since. But the Sox fell short again, this time to the Yankees. (*Below*) Ted stands by as Johnny Lindell's home run in the eighth frame of the final game, in New York, seals Boston's fate.

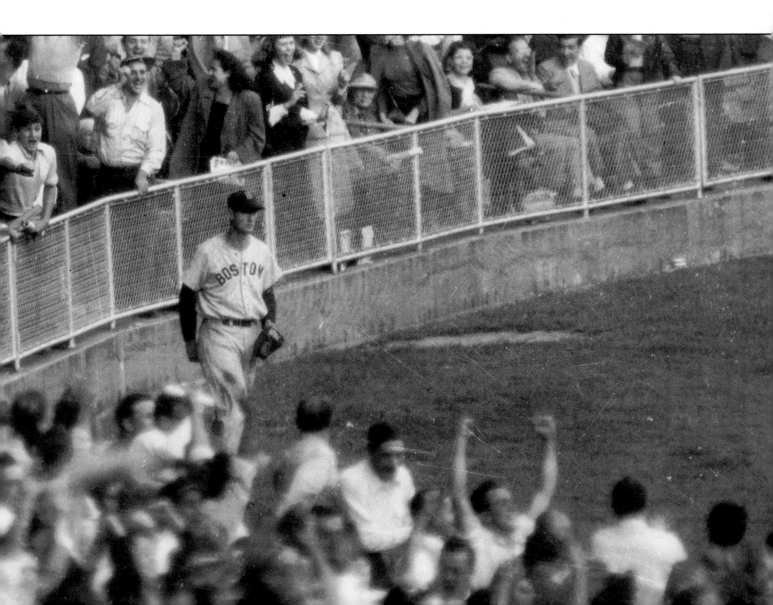

(*Clockwise from the near right*) While Ted was racking up stupendous records in the years after World War II, some interesting characters crossed his path. Hard-drinking Ellis Kinder, "Old Folks," became an overnight sensation for Boston at the age of thirty-five, wining 23 games for the luckless club of 1949. Manager Joe McCarthy had dealt with world-class carousers from Babe Ruth to Joe Page, but Kinder certainly led him a merry chase. Stan Musial may have been Ted's opposite number in the N.L. for pure hitting ability, but for home runs in the postwar period, Ralph Kiner was the major leagues' nonpareil, leading his league for seven straight seasons, 1946-52. He also hit the line drive in the 1950 All Star Game that Ted caught while shattering his elbow. George Kell nipped Ted for the 1949 batting title by the slimmest margin ever: .3429 to .3427. Both men finished with a .343 average, but Kell's two extra ten-thousandths of a point denied Ted a record third triple crown. Rip Sewell was renowned for his blooper pitch—the "eephus" ball—that came to the plate with so little velocity that no one had ever hit it for a homer. In the eighth inning of the 1946 All Star Game, Rip challenged Ted with an eephus that had a 20-foot arc; it sailed deep into the right field bleachers.

To Ted
a great ball
player and a
great guy for
Tom Yawkey

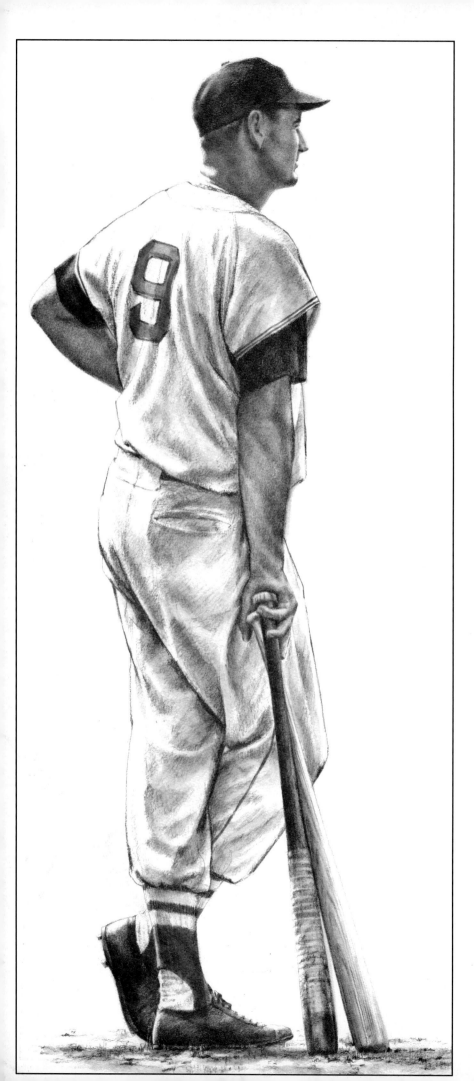

(*Overleaf, previous*) In a promotional shot of jaw-dropping inanity, Ted combines three of his lifelong interests. Falling for his line (or rising to his bait—it's tough to cast a true line in this metaphorical backwater) is the alluring Frances Plajnik, Arizona Queen of the "Anglers' World Series" of 1950. Flanked by Ted and jack of all trades Billy Goodman is Steve O'Neill, who took over as Red Sox manager in midyear when McCarthy decided to return home to Buffalo. O'Neill was the Kid's least favorite helmsman. Ted and Red Sox owner Tom Yawkey maintained a distant but mutual admiration society throughout his long association with Boston. (*Left, this spread*) Robert Riger's fine drawing of the Kid in repose. (*Right*) After his 1950 injury, Ted never again threw well, and he became a left fielder on whom runners could take liberties, especially on the road, where the walls were more distant. (*Overleaf, following*) Oh, how those Red Sox could hit! The final score of this game of June 8, 1950, against the St. Louis Browns was 29–4, with Boston's run total becoming the highest in this century. Of Boston's seven homers, Ted hit two.

The Kid's incredible exploits in his prime made him a hero, the darling of the fans if also their plaything. He rankled under the constraints and demands of a public life, but he was not immune to the siren song of celebrity. Sometimes he embraced its dark side, willingly transforming himself into a product.

THE KID IN FALL

Baseball in the 1940s had belonged to Ted. Starting out, he wrote in *My Turn at Bat*, "I had been a fresh kid. I did a lot of yakking, partly to hide a rather large inferiority complex." The rabbit ears and thin skin, not the swagger and bravado, genuinely reflected how the Kid saw himself. By mid-decade, feeling spurned and still no more comfortable with himself at the core, he stopped pursuing acclaim as if it were love and substituted the solitary pleasure that comes with achievement. He withdrew from the fans, which seemed only to heighten their ardor for him. Although he bade farewell to baseball repeatedly in the 1950s, each closing of the curtain proved only a prelude to a curtain call. The fans' thunderous applause would spur him to a glorious return, or Ted would discover that his thirst for the game had not been quenched, after all.

The great performances of the Kid's summer won him laurels; his fall, marked by comebacks from defeats and failings, inspired compassion and wonder. The hobbled hero could not help but see that the people were *for* him, no matter what. His troubles made him less different from them, more human, more lovable.

But was it too late? Would Ted, like his irascible teammate Lefty Grove, learn to say hello only when it was time to say goodbye?

> " The prevailing belief that Williams is swell-headed is entirely incorrect. The main trouble is that Ted suffers from an inferiority complex. He also admits he does things he shouldn't do, and doesn't do things he knows he should. 'Boston fans,' he said, 'were swell to me all through our [World] series at home, where I was a flop. I wanted to lift my cap to their applause. For some reason I couldn't do it. And I knew I was wrong.' "
>
> —*Grantland Rice, 1946*

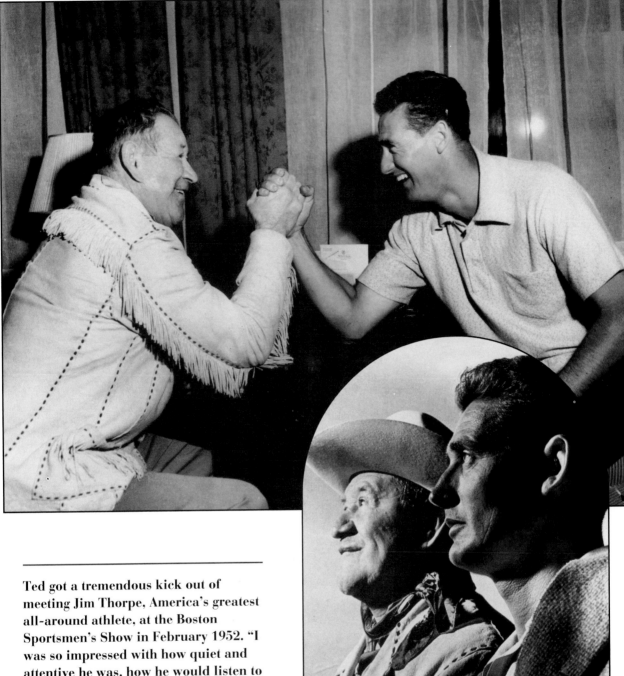

Ted got a tremendous kick out of meeting Jim Thorpe, America's greatest all-around athlete, at the Boston Sportsmen's Show in February 1952. "I was so impressed with how quiet and attentive he was, how he would listen to people." The big, easygoing Indian, who had known heights of adulation and depths of disappointment at least the equal of Ted's, had the gift. Ted had it, too, but only with children.

(*Above*) Lou Boudreau caused much gnashing of teeth in Boston in 1948. In 1952, however, he signed on to lead the Yawkey men. Ted knew before the season opened that as a Marine Reservist (and high-profile personality), he would be called to Korea. April 30 was proclaimed Ted Williams Day at Fenway and, with both he and the fans believing this would be his final game, the Kid capped the love fest with a game-winning homer in his last turn at bat. (*Overleaf*) And, for the only time between 1940 and 1960, he tipped his cap to the fans.

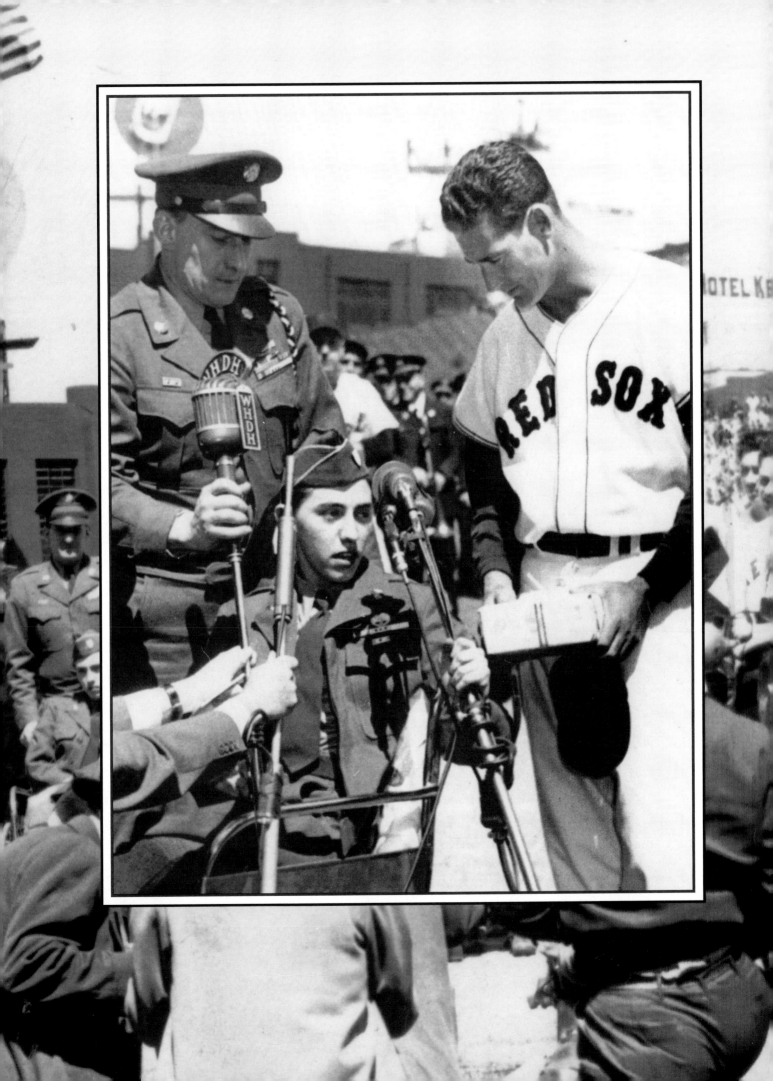

Ted flew F-9 Panther jets on thirty-nine bombing runs against North Korea in 1952–53. Returning from one of these, he was hit by enemy fire and lost his hydraulic and electrical systems. "Nothing worked. No dive brakes, flaps, nothing to slow the plane. I came barreling in at more than 200 miles per hour, fighting the stick all the way." Not knowing his tail was on fire, he hit the runway, sparks flying, and tore it up for 2,000 feet. He leapt from the cockpit before the fuel tanks burst. Shaken though he was, next day he was up in the air again.

Although he did his duty as a Marine without complaint, Ted was bitter about being recalled. In 1957 he created a stir by sharing his views (off the record, he thought) with a fellow Marine who happened to be a newspaperman. "A friend of mine was recalled for Korea," Ted said with indirection. "He knew Senator Taft. He asked Taft to help get him deferred. Do you know what Taft told my friend? Taft said, 'I can't touch you. You're pretty well known where you live. If you were just another guy, I'd be able to help you.' Now do you know why I think politicians are gutless?"

(*Above, right*) Williams was a dispirited, weak specimen by the time he was demobilized, beset with recurring viral infections and impaired hearing. (*Above, left*) Looking plum worn out, Ted wipes his brow salute-style after his first workout with Boston on July 30, 1953, only a day after his discharge from the Marines. Incredibly, his return to action produced this statistical line: 37 games, 91 at bats, 13 homers, 37 RBIs, and a slugging percentage of .901. (*Opposite, far right*) Williams went right to Fenway Park after his discharge, picking up the pedagogy where he last left it; here he advises Dick Gernert on the fine points of the basic tool. (*In oval*) Ted slid over from Gernert to greet Jimmy Piersall, the volatile center fielder who gave no quarter to Ted when it came to ragging. (*Near right*) Overseeing the whole scene was manager Lou Boudreau, whose shift from Cleveland to Boston was nearly as dramatic as the stacked defense he devised for the Kid back in 1946. (*Overleaf*) Ted was welcomed home by his favored charitable institution, the Jimmy Fund, at its August 1953 banquet.

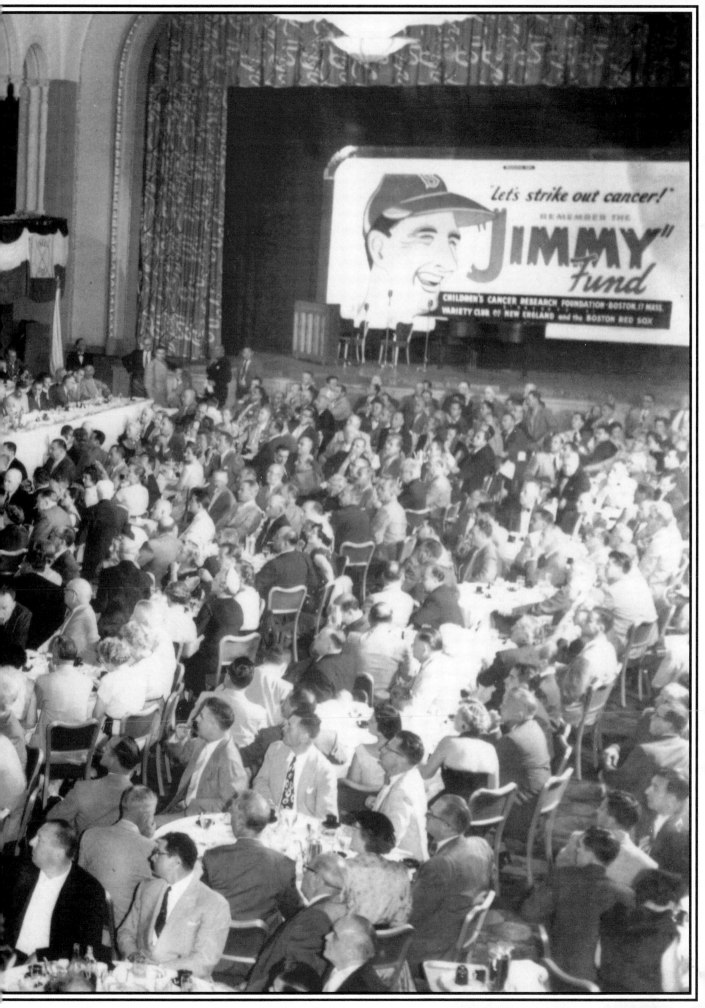

The celebrity bit wasn't *all* bad. Although Ted Kennedy gave a $50,000 check to Williams for the Jimmy Fund, it was the latter who won the kiss from movie starlet Elaine Stewart. And the Splendid Splinter got to hobnob with giants in other fields, like the similarly alliterative Slammin' Sammy Snead, who became his partner in a Miami fishing-tackle line.

(*Above, left*) Ted talks shop with another Williams boy—Cy Williams, a feared pull-hitter in the N.L. in the 1920s who may have been the first to face an overshifted defense like Boudreau's. Lou was replaced as Bosox manager after the 1954 season by Ted's former Red Sox third baseman Mike "Pinky" Higgins. The heart of Higgins' club would be his talented if temperamental outfield of Jimmy Piersall, rising star Jackie Jensen (*far left*), and Ted. Playing his first full season in three years, the Kid had broken his shoulder in spring training of 1954 and missed the early going, but showed he had not lost his zest or his eye by hitting .345 and drawing 136 walks. Critics complained that he would have been more valuable to his team by going after the bad balls, but it's hard to argue with a method that produced a lifetime on-base percentage of .483, the all-time record.

1955

...featuring exclusive article on batting by TED WILLIAMS

Famous Slugger Year Book

LOUISVILLE SLUGGER
BATS
HILLERICH & BRADSBY Cº
LOUISVILLE, KY.

Fishing became Ted's passion early on—it was a loner's sport, a way of replenishing the well of individuality that fuels creativity and vision. Fishing was purposeful like baseball, but not as intensely demanding. And it made for good friends, from the neighbor, Les Cassie, who had taken Ted fishing as a boy, to Sam Snead and Jimmy Albright and the Islamorada gang. At the time Ted and Doris divorced in Florida on May 9, 1955 (*left*), he had cast his lot (and his line) with the life of the full-time fisherman. Confronted with a stiff alimony settlement, however, on May 13 he unretired from baseball. He played in only 98 games that year but managed 28 homers and 83 RBIs to go with a batting average of .356.

Williams appeared in the Boston lineup for the first time in 1955 on May 23, in an exhibition game at Fenway against the world champion Giants (*right*). The Red Sox hopes for a flag in '55 were boosted by Ted's return but dampened by the early-season death of first baseman Harry Agganis (*above, right*). "The Golden Greek," a local boy and college-football hero, had played despite doctor's warnings; Ted cried at his memorial service in Washington.

Through all the seasons of the Kid,
his indelible essence was still
embodied in The Swing.

In 1956, once he began play after missing time with an arch injury, the Kid never missed a game. For the first time in five years, he amassed 400 at bats, the level required to compete for the batting championship that, on average alone, would have been his in 1954 and 1955. Although his fine .345 mark was a hit with the fans, this time it was not enough to win the title. Mickey Mantle (shown on the facing page, next to bat after Ted after a homer in the '56 All Star Game), finished at .353. The next year, however, would be Ted's "golden year"; the Mick would climb to .365 but be left in the dust as Ted hit .388. The golden year began with a rumor that Ted was about to marry a twenty-four-year-old actress named Nelva More (*right*). She confirmed the rumor to the press and the wedding bells were silenced.

(*Top*) Four .400 hitters: from the left, Bill Terry, Ted, Rogers Hornsby, and George Sisler. When the Kid hit .406 in 1941, the rule regarding sacrifice flies was to grant the batter an RBI but also to charge him with an at bat. Williams hit six scoring flies; remove those from his total at bats and his batting average would have been .411. In 1930, when Terry hit .401, at bats were not charged for fly balls that advanced runners to *any* base; Terry had 19 sacrifices that year, and one can safely presume that few if any were bunts. All this not only makes the .406 more impressive, but also the .388 of 1957. (*Center*) Even though Bobby Jo lived with Doris after the divorce, she and her dad still went fishing and occasionally she saw him play at Fenway. One night in 1957, when she was nine years old, Ted hit two homers for her. (*Bottom and opposite*) Still the top hitter in the game five years after he first thought the Korean War had finished his career, the Kid was accorded elder statesman status by all. Players like Mickey Vernon, an All Star himself, would gratefully accept his advice and manager Mike Higgins would defer to him about when he ought to play.

"The Splendid Spitter," or "Great Expectorations," or "The Night the Spit Hit the Fan"—the melodrama of August 8, 1956 was titled variously in the newspapers the next morning, but every writer agreed it was the worst thing they could remember a ballplayer ever doing on the field. After dropping Mickey Mantle's fly ball in the eleventh inning of a game at Fenway, Ted was booed. When he made a fine catch of a drive off the bat of Yogi Berra, the next batter, to end the inning, he was cheered. Fans! Ted spit to the left of them, spit to the right of them, and spit straight at them. As if this weren't bad enough, the game that evening was preceded by a celebration of Joe Cronin's induction into the Baseball Hall of Fame, and Cronin was present. Owner Tom Yawkey, aghast and angered, fined Ted $5,000. Ted was not apologetic in the least, but he did admit, "If I could stand a fine of $5,000 a day, I wouldn't be playing ball." The next day, he hit a home run and, as he crossed the plate, he clamped his hand over his mouth.

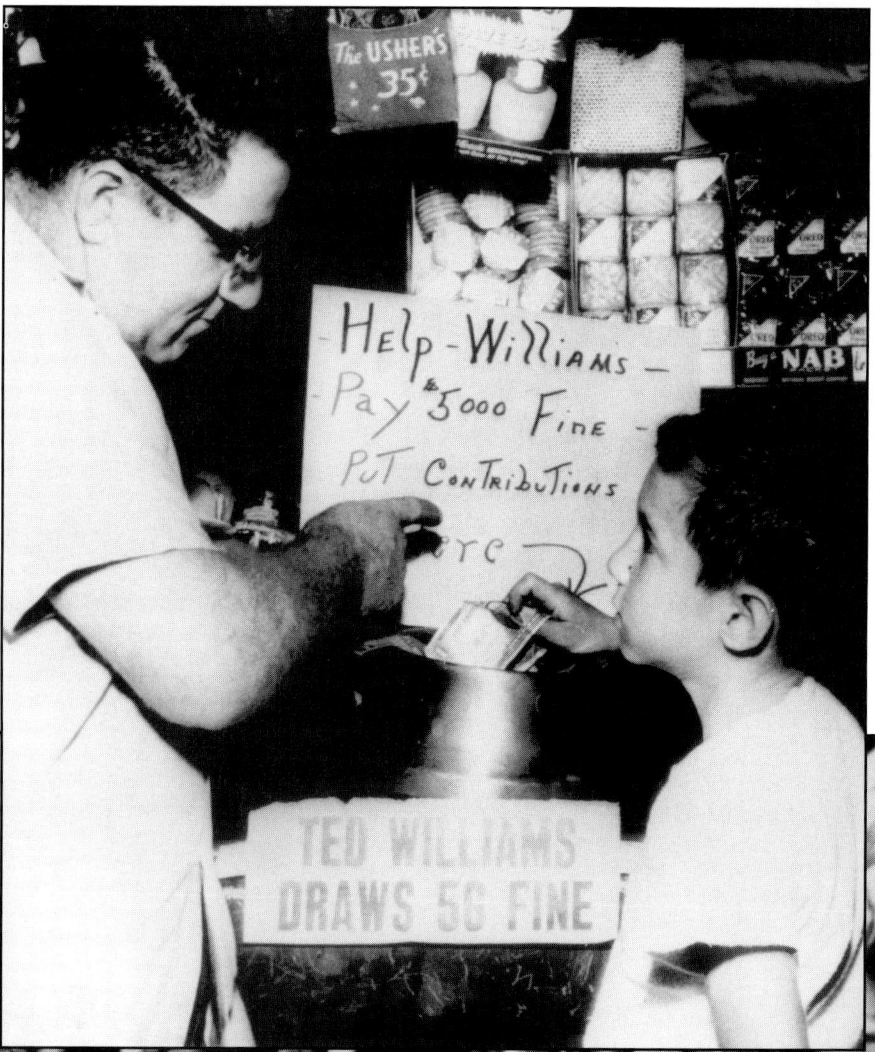
The USHER'S
35¢
-Help-Williams-
Pay $5000 Fine
Put Contributions
TED WILLIAMS
DRAWS 5G FINE

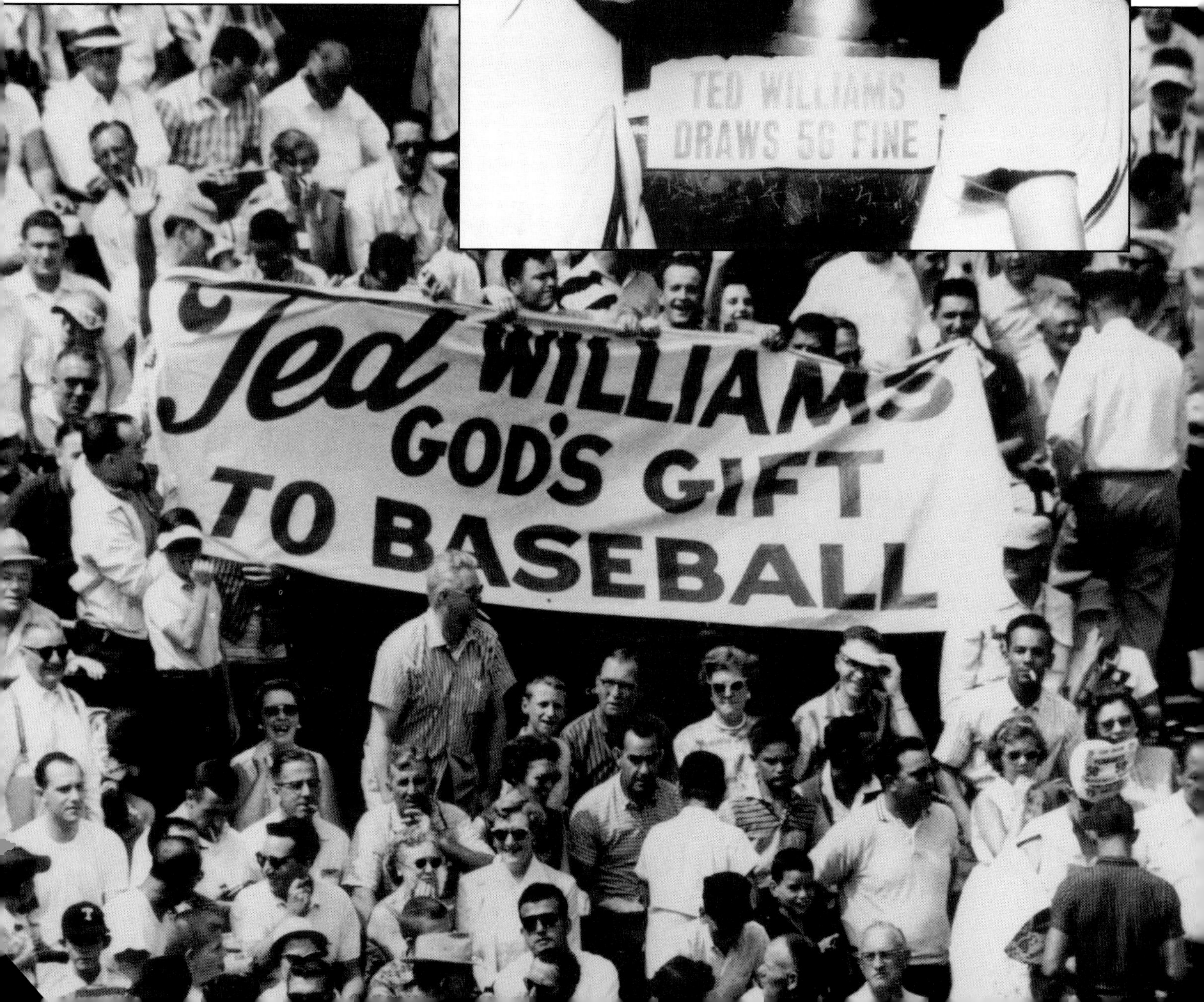
Ted WILLIAMS
GOD'S GIFT
TO BASEBALL

The day after Ted's salivary indiscretion, some fans set up brass spittoons as collection plates; a week later, all was forgiven. The Kid was still fulminating against front-runners, but the fans loved him anyway; there was nothing Ted could do to stop that now (although he wasn't through trying). (*Opposite*) Although Ted "slumped" sixty points in 1958 to hit .328, his sixth-inning double on the final day insured a batting-title victory over teammate Pete Runnels (*top*).

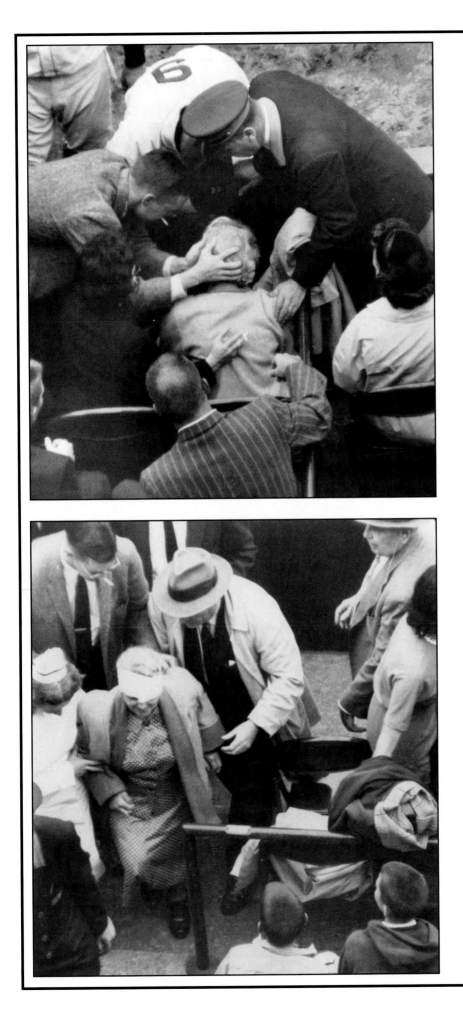

(*Opposite*) On September 20, 1958, locked in a nip-and-tuck battle with Runnels, Williams struck out with two men on. He flipped the bat away in disgust but the stickum on the bat handle caught on his fingers; the bat flew into the first row of seats, beaning Joe Cronin's housekeeper, Gladys Heffernan. Ted was horrified to see the bat sailing out of control, but relieved to learn that she was not seriously injured.

Be quiet; raconteur at work. Whether giving the reel scoop to a Little Leaguer or trading belting tips with boxer Carmen Basilio, advising the U.S. Senate on prospective legislation or just spinning a yarn for the boys, the Kid is no shrinking violet.

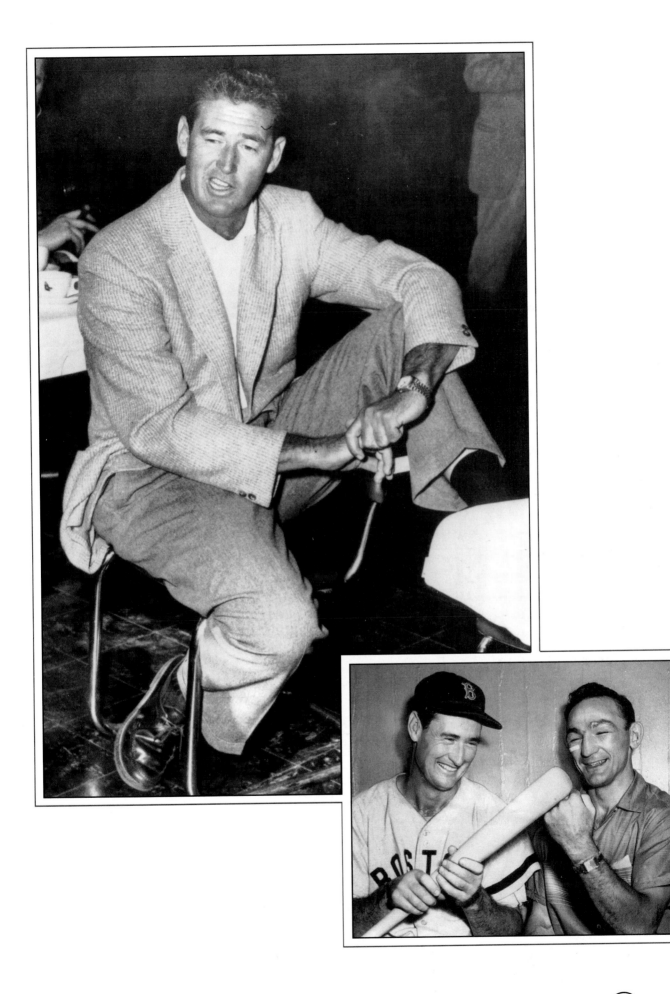

Williams and Musial were the best players in their leagues when Mickey Mantle came up in 1951. In later years Mantle said, "I don't think I consciously imitated any other player or athlete. But I guess I did try to acquire the general attitude of one other man. That man was Ted Williams. Ted showed me what it meant to be aggressive up there. He was the best I ever saw. Boy, when he swung, it wasn't any patty-cake, it was like he was out to *destroy* the ball."

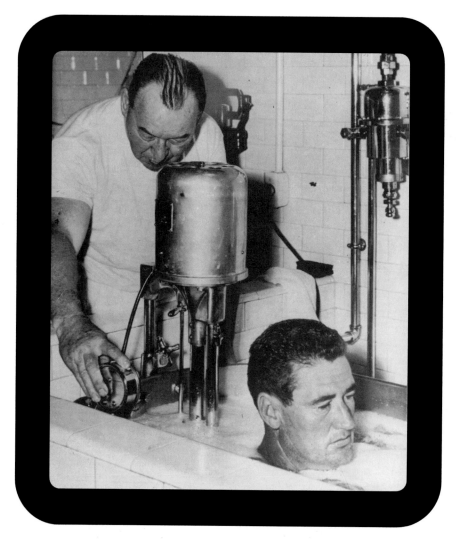

Time and again, the Kid came back from injury in the 1950s. The elbow in '50, pneumonia during the Korean War, the shoulder in '54, the arch injury in '56, and on and on. But nothing ever crippled Ted's performance like the pinched nerve in his neck in 1959. It limited him to under 300 at bats and an embarrassing batting average of .254. But he wasn't through. In 1960 he came back strong to hit .316, including his 512th home run to surpass the mark of Mel Ott. He traded the historic ball for a $1,000 check to the Jimmy Fund, a drop in the bucket compared to the $4 million he has raised over the years for children's cancer research.

1960

THERE IS A STRONG SHADOW OF DOUBT!

.Gallo.

BOSTON

TED

When Ted slipped in 1959, casting shadows over his prospects for '60, teammate Jackie Jensen (*opposite, left*) took up some of the slack, driving in over 100 runs for the second straight year. But when Ted returned to the fray in '60, Jensen retired, citing his inability to deal any longer with his fear of flying. Slugger Vic Wertz (*opposite, right*) was near the end of the trail when he came to Boston, but he squeezed out one last fine year in 1960, providing some protection behind Williams and collecting 103 RBIs. Ted shared a laugh at the second All Star Game of 1959 (in those years they played two) with Stan Musial and Willie Mays. He always believed that Willie, with all his speed, could have hit .400.

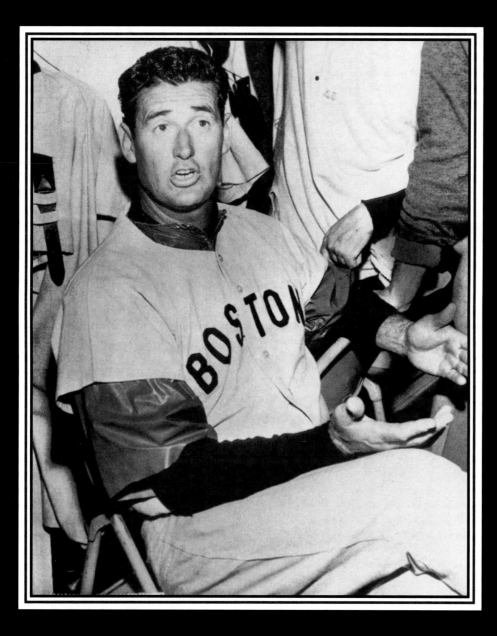

This is how 1960 began, with Ted telling reporters at the Red Sox spring camp in Scottsdale, Arizona, that if his neck acted up again he would have to hang up his spikes.

This is how 1960 neared its end, with Ted banging out home runs at his best clip ever and preparing to bow out at the top of his game.

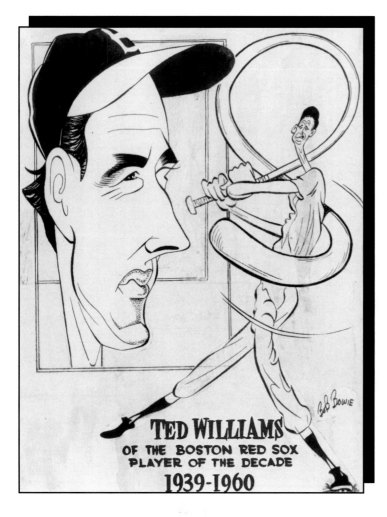

TED WILLIAMS
OF THE BOSTON RED SOX
PLAYER OF THE DECADE
1939-1960

The many moods of the Kid, all on display in his final season. Although 1951 was the only year in the decade in which Ted gathered more than 420 at bats, *The Sporting News* named him Player of the Decade. Clearly, this was a player for the ages.

The final at bat of the Kid's career, September 28, 1960. (*Opposite*) Ted takes the weighted practice bat from Willie Tasby, first man up in the eighth inning, and goes to the on-deck circle. Jack Fisher of the Orioles threw the first pitch low, then blew a slider by Ted; but his third pitch, a fastball, was crunched. Fighting the damp, heavy air, the ball sailed into the bullpen for a home run. Ted trudged around the bases, his cap in place, shook hands with on-deck batter Jim Pagliaroni, and the 10,454 fans roared in amazement. (*Overleaf*) Baltimore outfielder Al Pilarcik watches the ball fly out of reach, Ted says goodbye to Number 9, and Boston says goodbye to Ted.

Jensen Back With Red Sox in 1961

Ted Says It With 425 Ft. HR

(STORIES ON PAGE 36, OTHER PICTURES IN CENTERFOLD)

OLD FRIENDS—Mgr. Mike Higgins visits dressing room to greet Ted on his homer, while right behind is Judge Emil Fuchs, former pres. of the Boston Braves, also on hand to wish The Kid the best of luck as he departs as an active player. Ted will be back in '61 as a Sox batting instructor.

(Record Photo by Jim Phelan)

AU REVOIR—Ted, greatest modern batter, addressing the crowd of over 10,000 at Fenway before the game, in the presence of Mayor Collins, who presented Ted with a gift from the city. "My stay in Boston has been the most wonderful part of my life," Ted told the cheering fans.

LAST HURRAH—With the cheers of the throng ringing in his ears, Ted Williams ducks into the dugout after belting home run in the 8th inning of farewell game at Fenway Park yesterday. Applauding at the steps is Coach Del Baker, who is also retiring after the season.

(Record Photo by Myer Ostroff)

THE BIG ONE — Ted cuts loose on pitch by Orioles' Jack Fisher and sends ball soaring for 521st homer, the last of his career in eighth inning. O's Gus Triandos is behind the plate. The crowd started roaring at the crack of the bat as the famed slugger swung for the last time of his brilliant career with the Red Sox.

THE KID IN WINTER

The Kid was that rare individual for whom retirement at age forty-two was precisely right. He had orchestrated his exit perfectly, leaving the audience cheering. He was, if not rich, financially secure for the fairly modest demands he placed on life. Although descending from Mount Olympus to the valley peopled by mere mortals, he had in sight another mountain to climb: as he had become, by exercise of his will, the best hitter in the land, he would now become its best fisherman. And Ted was a curious man by nature, not the sort to sit idle; it is doubtful that he knew what it truly felt like to be bored, which is the most often cited peril of retirement.

Withdrawing from baseball in 1960 was the correct move, his body told him, but it was his mind that was most relieved at the prospect of retreating into the shadow from the glare of a life led, despite his wishes, in the open. A pensioned hero needed no one and nothing from his olden days: his story was written; he was complete unto himself.

The average fan might be excused for asking why a baseball god, who had been paid to *play*, after all, would ever want to take the pipe-and-slippers route. Sure, the reflexes slowed and the middle thickened, but why turn away from the public that had made you what you were? The answer for Ted was that the baseball life had never been easy, not any of it—from hitting a ball to giving an interview. For Ted it was never just play; it was always work, and he always worked under tremendous pressure—some of it self-imposed, as it is for all perfectionists, but much of it from the crowd and the press, whose readiness to leap upon him was real and relentless. He felt their slings and arrows so keenly because he needed their approval—everyone's approval—so deeply. After eight years of more or less private life, Ted felt eager for the limelight again.

> **"Ted Williams is a man of courage; he is a person; he is ever the master of a situation and never its slave."**
>
> *—Branch Rickey, 1965*

On September 18, 1961, Ted tried his hand at institutionalized domesticity once more, marrying model Lee Howard (shown at the right with designer Edith Head) in a Chicago courthouse. Like the Kid, his bride had been married before and hoped for better the second time around; a week after the ceremony, the couple was en route to the Miramichi River in New Brunswick for salmon fishing. Four years later they were headed downriver to divorce court.

Ted's long-term arrangement to promote and develop Sears sporting goods provided a good income and kept him in touch with the outdoors and kids, the two great loves that never failed to fulfill him. His summer camp for boys, specializing in baseball, became one of the most respected in the country. "He likes all children," Harold Kaese wrote of Ted, "and all children seem to like him. He acts their age. Grownups may say, 'Williams is a big kid,' but children do not hold that against him."

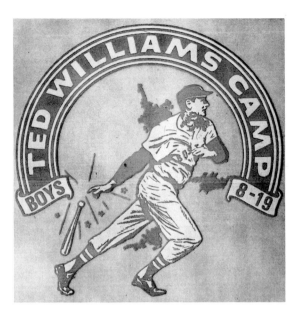

Ted's consulting role with the Red Sox included an annual appearance at spring training to provide batting instruction to prospects and major-league-roster performers. (*Below*) Ted shows how it's done to sophomore left fielder Carl Yastrzemski, in March 1962. Yaz would struggle for some time before attaining stardom. (*Right, top*) Whenever Ted returned to uniform in a coaching role, the urge to take a few swings was overwhelming, as was the fans' hunger for a glimpse of the legend in action. (*Right, bottom*) Batting coach Williams tells manager Pesky what he should do with the 1964 Red Sox—ship 'em out and get a real team.

(*Right*) Ted bagged the daily limit of two sharp-tailed grouse on a filmed hunting expedition to Ringgold, Nebraska, in 1963. The Baseball Hall of Fame operated under no such limit in 1966 when it tabbed two sharp-eyed grouse for its trophy room: the Kid and the Ol' Perfesser, Casey Stengel. In his brief but eloquent oration in Cooperstown, Ted thanked those who had helped him along the way, men like Eddie Collins, Frank Shellenback, Donie Bush, and others going all the way back to the years before he reached Boston. He also said, "Ballplayers are not born great. They're not born great hitters or great pitchers or managers, and luck isn't the big factor. No one has come up with a substitute for hard work."

Tension seethes outside the Miami courtroom where a judge is about to review the Williamses' divorce petitions. At the close of the hearing on August 12, 1965, the judge opined that reconciliation seemed possible, but in the end things didn't go that way. (*Overleaf*) When Ted talks hitting, *everyone* listens.

By 1968 the Splendid Splinter had splurged on the good things that came with a life of comparative idle. He was ready for a challenge, and Bob Short of the Washington Senators offered a deal the Kid couldn't refuse: a five-year contract to manage, with an option to buy 10 percent of the club. The appeal of Short's reward is plain on Ted's face in the photo below; the enormity of the challenge—Washington had not escaped the second division in the previous twenty-two seasons—seems on Ted's mind in the photo opposite.

Kids and the Kid, a pairing in which the chemistry was invariably right. Here Ted signs autographs for young fans for whom he is a legendary figure. (*Opposite*) The third Mrs. Williams relaxes at home in Islamorada in 1969. The former Dolores Wettach, whose love for the outdoors matched Ted's, had been Miss Vermont of 1956, an entrant in the Miss Universe competition, and a *Vogue* model. The couple had two children, John Henry and Claudia, before divorcing.

Ted's teaching went over so well with the Senators in his rookie year at the helm that the club went from 65 victories to 86. For Ted—whose patience with mediocre players had always been questioned—the startling improvement won Manager of the Year honors in the American League. The Kid was the toast of the town, popular on both sides of the congressional aisle. Here he shares a laugh with Speaker of the House John McCormack (D-Mass.) and Representative Gerald Ford (R-Mich.).

On April 23, 1969, The Kid made his first trip to Boston as manager of the
Senators and feigned fascination with the umpire's explanation of
Fenway's ground rules. Two years later, he grinned and bore the dismay he
felt at Bob Short's acquiring retread pitcher Denny McLain in exchange for
the left half of the Senators' infield. Ted knew his team would be
swimming upstream all season long.

In 1971 Washington's record was 63–96, worse than it had been in the year before Ted took the reins. Bob Short moved the club out of the nation's capital for 1972, and Ted followed along, becoming manager of the new Texas Rangers. Alas, the other teams were not fooled; they knew these guys may have had the eyes of Texas upon them, but they were still Senators at heart. Their won-lost record declined further, to 54–100 in the strike-shortened season. Ted began to recall how much cooler the summer was in New Brunswick than in Arlington.

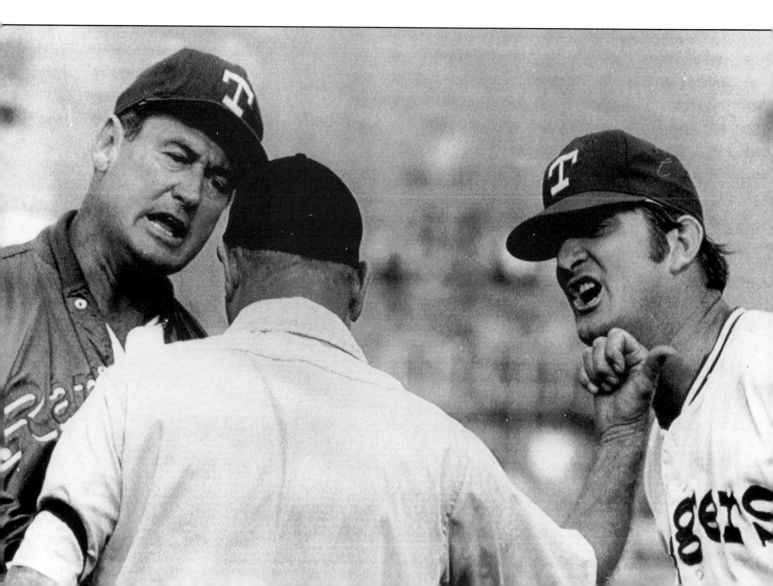

Bing Crosby (*opposite*), like Ted an ardent fisherman and private man, joined him at a 1971 banquet for the Committee to Save Atlantic Salmon. *Going My Way* had been the title of one of Bing's biggest film hits; the picket sign could have planted an idea in Ted's mind as to how save another endangered fighting spirit, his own. Let the salmon return to the Miramichi, and let the Kid go, too. On September 30, 1972 (*below*), the Rangers announced that Ted Williams would not be back for the fifth year of his contract.

In later years Ted enjoyed clowning with old friends like Jimmy Piersall at oldtimers' games and taking a swing or two. That and a bit of spring training was about as much baseball as he wanted now.

When Ted was young—even later, when he was in his prime—he couldn't wait to get to the ballpark, to wrap a bat in his hands. When Carl Yastrzemski came up to Boston in 1961, Ted saw a hitter cast from his own mold: waiting for the next pitch, he positively *quivered* with the scent of the prey. Even when age withered some of their skills, both Ted and Yaz retained the intensity, the appetite for challenge and the willingness to work, that made them great. The heart of the lion, the eye of the tiger, in a warrior these do not dim in honored age. Despite signs of mellowing and increasingly graceful acceptance of his baseball deity, Ted Williams is what he was: in all his tangled force and fury, the Kid.

TED WILLIAMS' BATTING RECORD

Note: league-leading figures are shown in bold, including Williams' marks in 1954, when he failed to qualify for official titles because he failed to register 400 at bats; in that year, however, he did have the 3.1 plate appearances per scheduled game that is the criterion for qualifiers today.

YEAR	TEAM/LEAGUE	G	AB	R	H	2B	3B	HR	RBI	BB	SO	BA	OBP	SLG	SB	CS
1936	San Diego-PCL	42	107	18	29	8	2	0	11	—	—	.271	—	.383	2	—
1937	San Diego-PCL	138	454	66	132	24	2	23	98	—	—	.291	—	.504	1	—
1938	Minneapolis-AA	148	528	**130**	193	30	9	**43**	**142**	114	75	.366	.481	.701	6	—
1939	Boston-A	149	565	131	185	44	1	31	**145**	107	64	.327	.435	.609	2	1
1940	Boston-A	144	561	**134**	193	43	14	23	113	96	54	.344	**.442**	.594	4	4
1941	Boston-A	143	456	**135**	185	33	3	**37**	120	**145**	51	**.406**	**.551**	**.735**	2	4
1942	Boston-A	150	522	**141**	186	34	5	**36**	**137**	**145**	51	**.356**	**.499**	**.648**	3	2
1943–5								(In Military Service)								
1946	Boston-A	150	514	**142**	176	37	8	38	123	**156**	44	.342	**.497**	**.667**	0	0
1947	Boston-A	156	528	**125**	181	40	9	**32**	114	**162**	47	**.343**	**.499**	**.634**	0	1
1948	Boston-A	137	509	124	188	**44**	3	25	127	126	41	**.369**	**.497**	**.615**	4	0
1949	Boston-A	155	566	**150**	194	**39**	3	**43**	**159**	**162**	48	.343	**.490**	**.650**	1	1
1950	Boston-A	89	334	82	106	24	1	28	97	82	21	.317	.452	.647	3	0
1951	Boston-A	148	531	109	169	28	4	30	126	**144**	45	.318	**.464**	**.556**	1	1
1952	Boston-A	6	10	2	4	0	1	1	3	2	2	.400	.500	.900	0	0
1953	Boston-A	37	91	17	37	6	0	13	34	19	10	.407	.509	.901	0	1
1954	Boston-A	117	386	93	133	23	1	29	89	**136**	32	**.345**	**.516**	**.635**	0	0
1955	Boston-A	98	320	77	114	21	3	28	83	91	24	.356	.501	.703	2	0
1956	Boston-A	136	400	71	138	28	2	24	82	102	39	.345	**.479**	.605	0	0
1957	Boston-A	132	420	96	163	28	1	38	87	119	43	**.388**	**.528**	**.731**	0	1
1958	Boston-A	129	411	81	135	23	2	26	85	98	49	**.328**	**.462**	.584	1	0
1959	Boston-A	103	272	32	69	15	0	10	43	52	27	.254	.377	.419	0	0
1960	Boston-A	113	310	56	98	15	0	29	72	75	41	.316	.454	.645	1	1
Total 19 years		2292	7706	1798	2654	525	71	521	1839	2019	709	.344	.483	.634	24	17

WORLD SERIES RECORD

YEAR	TEAM/LEAGUE	G	AB	R	H	2B	3B	HR	RBI	BB	SO	BA	OBP	SLG	SB	CS
1946	Boston-A	7	25	2	5	0	0	0	1	5	5	.200	.300	.200	0	0

Named American League Most Valuable Player, 1946, 1949
Named to American League All Star team, 1940–1942, 1946–1951, 1954–1960
Manager, Washington Senators, 1969–1971; Texas Rangers, 1972
Named to Hall of Fame, 1966

Best Wishes

Ted Williams

INDEX

PHOTO CREDITS

Beavercreek Branch Library
3618 Dayton-Xenia Road
Dayton, Ohio   45432